Śaivism

Some Glimpses

Contemporary Researches in Hindu Philosophy & Religion (ISSN 0971-9628)

1. Idealistic Thought in Indian Philosophy; by Shuchita C. Divatia (ISBN 978-81-246-0021-4)
2. Karma and Reincarnation: The Vedāntic Perspective; by Muni Narayana Prasad (ISBN 978-81-246-0022-1)
3. Stonemill and Bhakti: From the Devotion of Peasant Women to the Philosophy of Swamies; by Guy Poitevin and Hema Rairkar (ISBN 978-81-246-0059-7)
4. Śaivism: Some Glimpses; by G.V. Tagare (ISBN 978-81-246-0076-4)
5. Advaita: A Conceptual Analysis; by A. Ramamurty (ISBN 978-81-246-0067-2)
6. Mind–Body Dualism: A Philosophic Investigation; by Alpana Chakraborty (ISBN 978-81-246-0071-9)
7. Hinduism and Scientific Quest; by T.R.R. Iyengar (ISBN 978-81-246-0077-1)
8. Indra and Other Vedic Deities: A Euhemeristic Study; by Uma Chakravarty (ISBN 978-81-246-0080-1)
9. Brahma-Vāda: Doctrine of Śrī Vallabhācārya; by G.V. Tagare (ISBN 978-81-246-0112-9)
10. The Science of Enlightenment: Enlightenment, Liberation and God: A Scientific Explanation; by Nitin Trasi (ISBN 978-81-246-0130-3)
11. Retrieving Sāṁkhya History: An Ascent from Dawn to Meridian; by Lallanji Gopal (ISBN 978-81-246-0143-3)
12. The Philosophical Foundations of Hinduism; by A. Ramamurty (ISBN 978-81-246-0163-1)
13. The Eternal Hinduism; by Baidyanath Saraswati (ISBN 978-81-246-0249-2)
14. Vedānta and its Philosophical Development; by A. Ramamurty (ISBN 978-81-246-0347-5)
15. Sāṁkhya-Yoga Epistemology; by Mukta Biswas (ISBN 978-81-246-0371-0)
16. A Sourcebook of Classical Hindu Thought; by Arvind Sharma (ISBN 978-81-246-0643-8)
17. A Treatise on Advaita Vedānta; by S. Bhuvaneshwari (ISBN: 978-81-246-0707-7)
18. Advaita Metaphysics: A Contemporary Perspective; by Tapti Maitra (ISBN: 978-81-246-0747-3)
19. The Journey of Advaita: From the Ṛgveda to Sri Aurobindo; Priti Sinha (ISBN 978-81-246-0934-7)
20. Theory of Karma: As Interpreted in Brahmasūtra and Bhagavadgītā; by P. Jagannivas (ISBN 978-81-246-1054-1)
21. Fundamentals of Hindu Philosophy of Faith and Morals; by Girdhari Lal Chaturvedi (ISBN 978-81-246-1171-5)
22. Schools of Vaiṣṇavism; by P. Jagannivas and Dayanidhi Kozhiyalam (ISBN 978-81-246-1169-2 (Hb), (ISBN 978-81-246-1186-9 (Pb))

Contemporary Researches in Hindu Philosophy & Religion, no. 4

Śaivism

Some Glimpses

G.V. Tagare

DK PRINTWORLD®
Publishers of Indian Traditions

Cataloging in Publication Data — DK
[Courtesy: D.K. Agencies (P) Ltd. <docinfo@dkagencies.com>]

Tagare, Ganesh Vasudeo, author.
Śaivism : some glimpses / G.V. Tagare.
pages cm. – (Contemporary researches in Hindu philosophy & religion ; no. 4)
"First published in India in 1996"– Title page verso.
Includes bibliographical references and index.
ISBN 9788124600764 (HB)

1. Śaivism. 2. Hindu philosophy. I. Title. II. Series: Contemporary researches in Hindu philosophy & religion ; no. 4.

LCC BL1280.54.T34 2025 | DDC 294.5513 23

ISBN: 978-81-246-0076-4
First published in India in 1996
Second impression published in 2001
Third impression published in 2025

Printed and published by:
D.K. Printworld (P) Ltd.
Regd. Office: Vedaśrī, F-395, Sudarshan Park
(Metro Station: ESI Hospital), New Delhi – 110015
Phones: (011) 4172 2626, 98713 94815
e-mail: indology@dkprintworld.com
Website: www.dkprintworld.com

Preface

Śaivism is an ancient Indian religion in the broad sense of the term. It has millions of followers in all strata of the society all over India from Kedārnāth in the Himālayas down to Rāmeśvara in the south and from Paśupateśvara in Nepal to Somanāth on the western coast of the Arabian Sea.

It existed before the Indus (Sarasvatī?) civilization. The series of Śiva's names in the 'Rudrādhyāya' of the *Taittirīya Saṁhitā* (IV.5.7) and 'Śata-Rudriya', in the *Vājasaneyī Saṁhitā* (Ch. 16, 18) show that Śiva-worship is as old as the *Yajurveda*. Lord Kṛṣṇa's initiation in Paśupatism mentioned in the *Anuśāsana Parva* (14.379-380) of the *Mahābhārata* shows that it was a respectable sect of Śaivism in the fourth millennium BC, if the consensus of Brāhmaṇical *Purāṇas* on the date of Kṛṣṇa's death in 3101 BC (the very day on which *Kaliyuga* began) is to be believed. This ancient religion is still a living faith is shown in Günther-Dietz Sontheimer's *Pastoral Deities in Western India*. It is perhaps the only faith that continues to be so vibrant and popular that it continues to attract millions of pilgrims to the various sites sacred to Lord Śiva.

Śaivism is more than mere theology. It is a philosophy that keenly attracted the attention of ancient and modern sages and thinkers. With faith in Śiva as the Ultimate Reality, these sages pondered and meditated over Śiva deeply and expressed their speculations about the nature of Śiva (the Ultimate Reality). His relations with man and the world. Some glimpses about Śiva and His relations with man and world flashed before their "inward eye". These were recorded by them or by their disciples and we have a rich vista of Śaivism. Its philosophies, mythology rituals, etc.

It is neither possible nor necessary for a layman to enter into the intricate subtleties of the various doctrines promulgated by them. I propose to elucidate the main features of the following prominent schools of Śaivism:

(1) Pāśupatism;

(2) Kaśmīr Śaivism;

(3) Siddhānta Śaivism;

(4) Śivādvaita; and

(5) Vīra-Śaivism.

These schools are meant for decent people. They advise worship, *japa* (repetition of *mantra* in undertone), and *yoga* for the realization of Śiva and do not advise black-magic, reprehensible types of worship like the *Pañca Makāra Pūjā* (involving intake of wine, meat, sexual intercourse and the like). Those are *Vāmācāra* (left-handed) types of *Śaiva* sects. (As an instance see *Kāpālikas* pp. 132-35).

Curiously enough, the main tenets or broad features of these *Śaiva* (right-handed) schools are similar to those of some schools of Vaiṣṇavism. Thus the Monism of Kaśmīr Śaivism is similar to that of the *advaita* of Śaṅkara with the exception of the special type of his *Māyāvāda*. Siddhānta Śaivism, which is dominant in Tamil Nadu shares a number concepts of Duality (*dvaita*) with those of Madhva, the promulgator of *Vaiṣṇava* Dualism. Śrīkaṇṭha's *Śivādvaita* is akin to Rāmānuja's *Viśiṣṭādvaita*.

Not that these *ācāryas* borrowed from the other *Śaiva* or *Vaiṣṇava ācāryas*. That is totally against Indian (not merely Brāhmaṇical) tradition. In telling the Rāma story, a Śvetāmbara Jain author never borrows or mentions a

Digambara Jain predecessor. The similarity in the philosophical speculations of *Śaiva* and *Vaiṣṇava ācārayas* shows that great minds think alike. Call the ultimate Reality Śiva or Viṣṇu, thinkers thought in similar patterns called Monism, Dualism, etc. The spirit of syncretism so warmly espoused in *Purāṇas*, has expressed itself iconographically.

It is hoped that the wisdom of the old will prevail and may lead to social integration.

Śiva is the fountain-head of all arts according to *Purāṇas* like the *Vāyu* or *Brahmāṇḍa*. A peep through modern Art critics like A. Coomaraswami, Stella Kramarisch, H. Zimmer will convince anyone in the matter.

After deeply pondering over the problem, I believe that Śaivism has relevance in the present world of cut-throat competition and tremendous nerve-racking tensions. If one spares some time for *upāsanā* [worship, prayer meditation or some sort of communion with some spiritual entity, (call it Śiva, Viṣṇu, Śakti, etc.)] one can gain some peace of mind, and poise and successfully cope with one's job, however intricate or difficult it may be. 'Have faith in me and do your duty conscientiously' — this message of *Karma-Bhakti Samuccaya* shows the relevance of Śaivism to the present age.

I sincerely thank Shri Susheel K. Mittal, Director of the D.K. Printworld, New Delhi, for his kind encouragement and forbearance shown to this aged author. This beautiful production of this book is due to him and his associates.

I also thank the artist for the sublime presentation of Lord Śiva. Lastly, I thank the Librarian of Shivaji University, Kolhapur, for providing me the references promptly.

Hope this last *bilva* leaf will please the gracious Lord Śiva to whom this work is dedicated.

G.V. Tagare

Contents

Abbreviations

BG — *Bhagavadgītā*

BMB — *Brahma-Mīmāṁsā-Bhāṣya*

BrS — *Brahma Sūtra*

ChāUp — *Chāndogya Upanṣad*

KŚ — *Kāśmīr Śaivism*

Mbh — *Mahābhārata*

Pāś — *Pāśupata*

PP — *Periya Purāṇa*

ṚV — *Ṛgveda*

ŚA — *Śivādvaita*

Saṁ — *Saṁhitā*

ŚB — *Śrīkara Bhāṣya*

SP — *Saṁbandhara Purāṇa*

SŚ — *Siddhānta Śaivism*

SŚn — *Siddhānta Śikkāmaṇi*

ŚV — *Śakti-Viśiṣṭādvaita*

ŚvUp — *Śvetāśvatara Upaniṣad*

TaittSaṁ — *Taittirīya Saṁhitā*

TaittĀr — *Taittirīya Āraṇyaka*

TaittUp — *Taittirīya Upaniṣad*

TD — *Tattvārtha Dīpikā*

TP — *Tattvārtha Prakāśa*

TM — *Tirumandiram*

VāiSaṁ — *Vājasaneyi Saṁhitā*

VŚ — *Vīra-śaivism*

Introduction

What is Śaivism

Śaivism is a school of Indian Philosophy which believes that there is some ultimate principle —*para tattva* : at the basis of the universe, which, within itself, creates, sustains and withdraws within itself (annihilates) the universe. It believes : that principle is both immanent and transcendent to the universe. For the sake of the convenience of linguistic expression, it is called "Śiva" (the Auspicious). Hence the school came to be designated as *Śaiva* (Śaivism).

The school speculates about the nature of Reality called Śiva (or *pati* in the jargon of Śaivites), its relation with the Individual Soul (*jīvātman* or *paśu* in Śaivite jargon) and with the world at large and among themselves. When you designate this ultimate Principle as Viṣṇu (the pervader of the universe), it is Vaiṣṇavism. It is, however, interesting to note that the speculations of both these — **isms** about the nature of the Reality or the Ultimate Principle, the individual soul and the world, run in certain similar thought-patterns. Broadly speaking, the school or thought pattern which believes that the Ultimate Reality and the Individual Soul are one (or equal) may be called Monists or *Advaitins* or *Īśvarādvaya-Vādins* (holding non-difference between God and man).

This is a very broad statement as there are several differences between both these schools. For the sake of brevity and simplicity we shall mention *Īśvarādvaya-Vāda* as *Kashmir Śaivism* (KŚ). When God, individual souls and objects in the world are regarded as different mutually and *inter se*, that school is called *dvaitin* or Dualist. Madhva was the exponent of Vaiṣṇava Dualism. The Śaiva Dualists are known as *Śaiva Siddhāntin*s and their school, *Siddhānta Śaivism* (*SŚ*). Though this school originated in Kashmir and was dominant up to AD 800, it shifted to Madhya Pradesh in the tenth century AD. King Bhoja of Dhar (AD 1018-60), a patron of this school, has contributed to its philosophy. At present Tamil Nadu is its stronghold. The credit of establishing it here goes to Śaiva Tamil Saints and authors like Aghora-Śiva (AD 1200).

There is a third thought-pattern about the relation between God, Man and the world. It believes that the individual soul (a conscious entity, *cit*) has a sort of qualified identity with God (be he Śiva or Viṣṇu) and the world (unconscious — *a-cit*) has a qualified relation with God. A sort of identity — "qualified non-duality" is posited between God, Man and the world. Hence it came to be known as *Viśiṣṭādvaita*. Rāmānuja is the Vaiṣṇava exponent while the Śaiva promulgator of this doctrine is Śrīkaṇṭha. Another very powerful group of this type is Vīraśaivism who advocate *Śakti-Viśiṣṭādvait*s.

Though these Śaiva and Vaiṣṇava schools are broadly clubbed together as Monists, Dualists etc., there are very important differences in Śaiva and Vaiṣṇava schools. We shall consider here the most important Śaiva schools viz:

(1) Kashmir Śaivism (KŚ)

(2) Siddhānta Śaivism (SŚ)

(3) Śivādvaits or Śrīkaṇṭha's schools (ŚA)

(4) Śakti-Viśiṣṭadvaits (ŚV) or Vīra-Śaivism

These are originally based on Śaiva *Āgama*s.

There is a Vedic School of Śaivism called *Pāśupatism*. Though it shares the fundamental concepts of Śaivism along with others, it is treated separately as it is non-Āgamic.

Cultural Contribution of Śaivism

Śaivism is not a dry philosophy. Its cultural contribution is a superb fusion of Art and Philosophy. Kroeber and Kluckhohn have recorded more than one hundred and sixty formal definitions of culture in *Culture: A Critical Review of the Concepts and Definitions*[1]. But instead of going into the complexities of those definitions, I would like to adopt an earlier definition by Sir E.B. Tylore[2] who describes culture as "that complex whole which includes knowledge, belief, art, morals, laws, customs and other capabilities, acquired by man as a member of the society". Literature or literary aspect of Śaivism, the glory and legends of Lord Śiva sung in epics, (*Mahākāvyas*), *Purāṇas*, dramas, *stotras* (eulogies and prayers) is already familiar to all and are adequately appreciated by literary critics. I would like to present just a glimpse of the Art-aspect of Śaivism.

Śaiva Art is not flippant. It is pregnant with *Vedānta*, *Bhakti* with its intensely appealing lyricism and such other serious concepts. But they are presented in such an attractive form as conveys its message to a common man without his being aware of it.

Let me take up the art of dancing. In the bronzes of the Cola period of the tenth century AD or those of Tanjore of the twelfth century AD, Indian artists have conceived of the cosmic rhythm in the most imaginative and symbolic manner in the icon of Dancing Śiva (Naṭarāja). Śiva ia traditionally regarded as the Lord of Dancing. The eternal rhythm of evolution (*sṛṣṭi*) and destruction (*pralaya*) of the universe is exquisitely expressed. Ananda Coomaraswamy explains the famous image of Naṭarāja: "The upper hand of the God holds a *ḍamaru* to sumbolize the primal musical *Nāda* of creation. The mystic experience of a Tibetan Lama noted by Mrs. Alexandra David in her *Tibetan Journey* is interesting. The Lama told her :

> All things are aggregrate of atoms — each atom perpetually sings its song and the sound at every moment creates dense and subtle form.

A. Coomaraswamy continues (about Naṭarāja):

> The upper left hand bears a tongue of a flame, fire, the element of destruction. The balance of these two hands, represents the dynamic balance of creation and destruction.

It is further accentuated by Śiva's calm and detached face in the centre of those two hands in which the polarity of creation and destruction is dissolved and transcended.

The second right hand is raised to express (*abhaya mudrā* — the gesture "do not fear"). It symbolizes maintenance and protection of the universe and peace. The remaining hand points down to the uplifted foot. It symbolizes release from the illusion of *māyā*. Śiva is shown as dancing on the body of a demon — the symbol of man's ignorance. It must be annihilated before the attainment of *mokṣa* (Liberation from *Saṁsāra* — *Dance of Śiva*).

Another eminent art critic, Heinrich Zimmer says about *Dancing Śiva*,

> His gestures wild and full of grace, precipitate the cosmic illusion. His flying arms and legs and the swaying of his torso produce — indeed they are — the continuous creation, destruction of the universe, death exactly balancing birth, the annihilation, the end of everything coming forth.[3]

A.L. Basham calls it "the greatest and most triumphant achievement of bronze casting".[4]

This cosmic dance of Śiva, in a way, represents the scientific reality in sub-atomic world as discovered by Modern Physics. Dr. Fritjof Capra who had been doing research in theoretical high energy Physics in the universities of Paris, California and Stanford has contributed many papers about the relation between modern Physics and Oriental mysticism. His book, *The Tao of Physics*[5] is an exploration of the parallels between Modern Physics and Eastern Mysticism. Capra says, "For the Modern Physicist, then Shiva's dance is the dance of sub-atomic matter... The bubble-chamber photographs of interacting particles, which bear testimony to the continual rhythm of creation and destruction in the universe, are visual images of the dance of Shiva equalling those of Indian artists in beauty and significance". (p. 259)

The metaphor 'cosmic dance' thus unifies ancient mythology, religious arts and modern Physics. It is indeed, as Coomaraswamy says, "Poetry but non-the-less-science".

The cultural influence of Śaivism is not limited to performing arts but extends to architecture and sculpture, but I have taken up this image of Dancing Śiva at first as Dr. Kapila Vatsyayana says, "Over a period of 2000 years, the image of Dancing Śiva has fascinated, the poet, the sculptor, the painter, the musician, while Indian drama and poetry, sculpture and painting have immortalised these eternal myths, it is Indian performing arts which have provided a living link into contemporary times".

It is not merely the icon of Śiva but we have the use of beautiful female forms, scantily dressed, as a decorative motif. The Indian artist is not averse to sensuous beauty, though he expresses Vedāntic concepts symbolically as in the case of dancing Śiva. The floral embellishment on door-frames and columns in temples is simply superb.

Śiva is associated with music both vocal and instrumental. The *Vāyu Purāṇa* gives a list of nine musical instruments such as *bherī* (war-drum), *ḍiṇḍima*, *jharjhara*; *dundubhi*; wind-instruments like *veṇu* (flute), *gomukha*; string instruments like *tuṁbevīṇā* (i.e., *tānpūrā*). Some of these are not mentioned in the *Ṛg Veda* but Śiva's followers of lower status like *bhūtas* play on them. Just as many *rāgas* and *rāginīs* bearing local or provincial names such as Gurjarī, Karnāṭakī, Bangālī[6] etc. show their base in local folksongs.

A visit to some ancient temples and prominent museums will convince anyone about the great cultural contribution of Śaivas.

Notes

1 Peabody Museum of American Archaeology and Ethnology, Harvard University Papers XLVII, No. 1, pp. 1-223.
2. Tylore E.B. : *Primitive Cultures*, New York, 1874.
3. *Myths and Symbols in Indian Art and Civilization*, Princeton University Press 1972, p. 155.
4. *The Wonder that was India*, p. 575.
5. Fontana/Collins, 1976.
6. *Skanda Purāṇa* — *Nāgara Khaṇḍa*, chs. 254, 27-45.

Curiously enough the position of the main *rāgas* is located with particular Yogic *cakras* or Plexuses.

Todays' classical Hindu Music is based on or evolved from folk-music and not so much from *sāma-gāna*.

Śiva is a *mahā-naṭa*. In the *Skanda Purāṇa* (VI. 254.28-45) we are told that when Śiva began to dance, six *rāgas* with their wives (*rāginīs*) assumed human forms and accompanied Śiva in his dance. The *rāgas* and their wives (*rāgiṇīs*) are named as follows:

	Name of the Rāga	*Name of Corresponding Rāgiṇīs*
1.	Srī	(1) Gaurī, (2) Kalāhalī, (3) Dhīrā, (4) Drāviḍī, (5) Mālakauśiki, (6) Devagandhā
2.	Vasanta	(1) Āndolā, (2) Kauśikī, (3) Carama-Mañjirī, (4) Gaṇḍagiri, (5) Deva-śākhā, (6) Rāmagirī
3.	Pañcama	(1) Triguṇā, (2) Staṁbhatīrthā, (3) Ahirī, (4) Kumkumā, (5) Vairāṭī, (6) Sāmavedī
4.	Bhairava	(1) Bhairavī, (2) Gurjarī, (3) Bhāṣā, (4) Velāṅgulī, (5) Karṇāṭakī, (6) Rakta-haṁsā
5.	Megha (Malhāra)	(1) Bangālī, (2) Madhurā, (3) Kāmodā, (4) Akṣinārikā, (5) Devagirā, (6) Devātī
6.	Naṭa-Nārāyaṇa	(1) Troṭakī, (2) Modakī, (3) Narā, (4) Duṁbī,(5) Malhārī, (6) Sindhu-Malhārī

The names of provinces like Gurjara, Karnataka etc. show that they were developed out of local folk-music.

The Positions of Rāgas in Yogacakras

	Name of the Cakra	*Name of the Rāga*
1.	Bhrū-madhya	Śrī
2.	Mūlādhāra	Vasanta
3.	Viśuddhi	Pañcama
4.	Anāhata	Bhairava
5.	Maṇipūra	Megha
6.	Ādhāra	Naṭa-Nārāyaṇa

Though the *Purāṇa* is not a work on musicology, it is enough to show the belief of Śiva being the progenitor of vocal music.

1

Some Fundamental Concepts

Śaivism whether Vedic or Āgamic, shares some common fundamental concepts and technical terms. They are *pati*, *paśu* and *pāśa*. These terms have been used by the ancient-most Śaiva sect called *Pāśupatism* or *Pāśupata-mata*. The founder of this sect is "La (Na)-kulīśa". He was regarded as the twenty-eighth incarnation of Śiva (*Śiva Purāṇa* : *Vāyavīya Saṁhitā* 2.9.5, *Kūrma Purāṇa*, I.53). His historicity has been established inscriptionally. His work — The *Pāśupata Sūtra* (*Pāś. S*) has come down to us with an excellent commentary by Kauṇḍinya (*circa* fifth century AD).

Pati in Pāśupatism

According to Pāśupatas and other Śaiva sects, *pati* is Śiva (The Auspicious). The word *pati* is derived from √*pā*- 'to protect'. Śiva creates and protects all beings including god Brahmā. Kauṇḍinya in *Pāś. S*, 5. defines:

Śiva is designated as *Pati*, as He creates and protects Paśus (beings).[1] He is one, eternal. It is due to His Grace (*anugraha*) that beings can attain *Mokṣa* (release from *Saṁsāra*). One cannot achieve *Mokṣa* on the strength of one's individual knowledge or renunication.[2]

This is obviously an echo of the *Kaṭha Upaniṣad* (*Kaṭha Up.*) which declares that realization of the Self (*ātman*) depends solely on His Grace.[3] Śiva is the material and instrumental cause of the universe.

Pati in *KŚ*

There is another school of Śaivism, based on ancient *Śaiva Āgamas*. Its founder, Vasugupta (*circa* AD 825) belonged to Kaśmir, hence the school is popularly known as Kaśmir Śaivism (*KŚ*). Its basic text is *Śiva Sūtra*. It is believed that it was disclosed to Vasugupta by Śiva Himself in his dream. It advocates non-difference between Śiva, individual Soul, and the universe. Hence this doctrine is called *Īśvarādvaya-Vāda* (for the sake of brevity Kaśmir Śaivism is mentioned as *KŚ*). According to *KŚ Pati* is the Supreme Śiva (*Para Śiva*). He is the ultimate Principle. Its synonyms are: *cit*, *citi*, *parā saṁvit* (Ultimate consciousness or knowledge), *Parameśvara* (Supreme Ruler). The concept of *Para Śiva* in *KŚ* is superior or more comprehensive than that of the *sañkarita Brahman*.

Para Śiva is beyond name or form. He is both immanent and transcendant to the universe. The universe is *Pati*'s manifestation within Himself. He is endowed with *prakāśa* (Supreme Knowledge) and *vimarśa* (power to create, to sustain, to destroy anything by sheer will-power, without the help or assistance of any outside agency like *māyā*, *avidyā* and the like) *KŚ* argues that if *Pati* be presumed as being without this *vimarśa* power. He would be *jaḍa* (inert) like a stone or a clod of earth.[4]

The Dualists' View

The other important but Dualistic school is *Siddhānta Śaivism* (*SŚ*). It appears that it originated in Kaśmir and was older and more popular than the school of Vasugupta. Vasugupta's followers had to popularise their sect by claiming Śiva as the real author of the *Śiva Sūtra* and Vasugupta was only a medium to propagate Śiva's philosophy.[5]

The eldest extant author of this Dualistic school is *Sadyojyoti* (*c.* ninth century AD). In his *Kārikās* he accepts *Pati*, *Paśu* and *Pāśa* as fundamental concepts. For example, in the first verse of the *Tattva-traya-nirṇaya*, he pays obeisance to Śiva calling Him *Pati* who is independent, beginningless, granter of fruits of *karmans* to all beings impartially.[6] At the same time he confirms the co-status of the individual soul (*puruṣa*) with Śiva.[7]

This school is now very popular in Tamil Nadu and not in Kaśmir.

Another famous school of Śaivism of the *Viśiṣṭādvaita* type is called *Śivādvaita*. Its famous exponent is Śrīkaṇṭha. Like previous *ācāryas* of other school he tried to establish his view in his *Brahma-mīmāṁsā bhāṣya* (*BMB*) — a commentary on the *Brahma Sūtra* (*Br.S*). His commentary takes a stand similar to that of Rāmānuja in *Śrībhāṣya* though at some places he leans to the *Advaita* of Śaṅkara.

His acceptance of *Br. S.* as the authoritative text, forced Śrīkaṇṭha to declare that Śiva and *Brahman* are synonymous and Śiva's position in *KŚ* is compromised. According to *BMB* Śiva is the subtle cause. It is characterised both by *Cit* (consciousness, knowledge) and *acit* (*jaḍa*, non-consciousness). The subtle *cit* and *acit*, to quote *BMB* "*The Brahman charcterised by subtle Cit* and *Acit* is the cause.[8] As the Upaniṣadic *Brahman* and Śiva are identical, Śiva is described as being endowed with infinite suspicious characteristics".[9]

Śrīkaṇṭha repeats the identity of Śiva with *Brahman* in so many places in *BMB*.

Another school, very powerful in Karnataka, is *Vīra Śaivism* or *Śakti-Viśiṣṭādvaita*. Its exponent was Śrīpati

Paṇḍit, a brāhmaṇa from Andhra (*circa* AD 1100). His lucid commentary on the *Br. S.* is well-known as *Śrīkara Bhāṣya*. It is amusing to find that both Śrīkaṇṭha and Śrīpati are valiantly trying to show that Āgamic Śaivism has the firm support of the *Br. S.* though not all Śaivas had a special respect for *Br. S.* I call Śaṅkara a *Vaiṣṇava* as his *guru-paraṁparā* starts from Viṣṇu as follows:

Viṣṇu . . . . . . Brahmā . . . . . Nārada . . . . . Śuka . . . . Gauḍapāda Govind Yati. As Śaṅkara is not a Śaiva, his views are excluded here.

Vīra Śaivism regards this Śiva or *Pati* as the same as Upaniṣadic *Brahman*. They assert the equality between the *Vedas* and *Āgamas* as Śiva is the author of both these works. They claim that the *Br. S.* advocates their philosophy viz; *Śakti-Viśiṣṭādvaita*.

Paśu (Individual Soul)

All Śaiva sects use the term *Paśu* for the individual soul. The other synonyms used for *Paśu* are : *aṇu*, *ātmā*, *jīva*, *pudgala*, *kṣetrajña*.

The *Liṅga Purāṇa* explains that individual souls from god Brahmā downwards are called *Paśus* of the God of *Devas* (Śiva) as they are bound down by *Saṁsāra*. As Śiva is their master, He is called Paśupati.[11] It is noteworthy that no sect of Śaivism regards *jīvātman* (individual soul) as the 'creature' of Śiva. Śrīkaṇṭha on *Br.S.*, 2.3.18 (*Ātmādhikaraṇa*) plainly states :

> Individual souls are not created or born.[12]

In other words Śiva and *jīvātman* are of the same status, though the original powers of *jīva* are closely circumscribed or limited by *malas* or *pāśas* so much so that from the point of powers, *jīva* is like an atom as compared with Śiva. The term *aṇu* for *jīva* is not used in a spatial sense. When the *malas* are completely washed off or the bonds (*pāśas* are cut asunder, the *jīvātman* attains his original Śiva-hood. Consciousness (*caitanya*) is the common factor between *jīva* and Śiva.

The term *paśu* for *jīvātman* seems to be first adopted by the oldest and *Veda*-based sect called *Pāśupatism*. Kauṇḍinya in his commentary on the *Pāśupata Sūtra* (*Pāś. S.*) quotes from the *Pañcārtha-bhāṣya* :

> With the exception of those who are liberated through *Sāṅkhya* or are The Masters (experts) in *Sāṅkhya-Yoga* all beings from god Brahmā are *Paśus*.[13]

The individual souls are encaged in *Puryaṣṭaka* (a City consisting of 'eight' viz. five *tanmātras* (subtle elements) plus the psychical apparatus viz. *buddhi* (intellect), *ahaṁkāra* (Ego, Sense of I-ness), *manas* (mind). The other term used by other schools is *Liṅga-Śarīra*.

The term *Puryaṣṭaka* is adopted by *Siddhānta Śaivas* (*SŚ*) as is seen from Bhojadeva's explanation in the *Tattvārtha Prakāśa* (*T. Pr.*).[14] Bhojadeva and Śivādvaitin Śrīkaṇṭha hold that the individual soul and his cage (*Puryaṣṭaka*) are transferred to the next birth of the Individual Soul. The size of the body of the previous birth and the next birth may be different (as that of an ant and an elephant), the *Puryaṣṭaka* occupies the whole body like a lamp filling the whole room with light irrespective of the size of the room.[15]

Pāśa or *Mala*

All sects of Śaivism explain that though *jīva* and Śiva are of equal status and possess the same powers originally, the powers of the *jīva* are restricted due to the limiting factor called *pāśa*, *bandha*, *mala*, *ajñāna*, *paśutva*, *tamas* or *avidyā* — all synonyms for Ignorance.[16] There are, however, some slight differences in the implications of each, but they are grouped together as each of these is, as per usage of different Śaiva writers, a limiting factor.

But by 'Ignorance', Śaivas do not mean 'total absence of knowledge' or 'Total ignorance' but only a partial one. They say that the concept of total ignorance will reduce the individual soul whose special characteristic *sin-qua-non* is *caitanya*, to the category of a stone or a clod of earth.[17] The problem, however, is that if *jīva* and Śiva are equal in status, how is it that the *jīvātman* got 'soiled' with *mala* (dirt) or got enchained in *pāśa* at all. No Indian philosopher (believing in God or the Soul) has a satisfactory reply. Śaivas attribute it to the will power of *Parama Śiva* which drastically restricted the powers of the *jīva* and made him an atom — an imponderable willfulness of the great Śiva! This consciousness of imperfection creates an innate limitation,[18] in that *aṇu* (*jīva*) and is hence called *āṇava mala* (the innate *mala* of an *aṇu* or *jīva*). This *mala* is beginningless but it ends in the *mokṣa* stage.

This concept of *mala* is different from the *rāga* concept of *Sāṅkhyas*. They regard *rāga* as the quality of intelligence (*buddhi*) which creates attachment.

As noted above, all *Śaiva* sects believe that Ignorance of a *jīva* is partial and not total. It is 'slight knowledge' as *BMB* puts it. This *āṇava mala* makes the *jīva* believe in the identity of the body and the Soul (*dehātmaikya-bhāve*). It is only in the *mokṣa* stage that this *mala* is washed off completely.

KĀRMA MALA

Kārma mala is confused by some with *karma saṁskāra*. But *saṁskāras* are the effects of mental, verbal and physical acts committed by a *jīva*. *Kārma mala*, however, is objectless limited will-power of the Soul and its existence depends on the innate ignorance called *āṇava mala*.

In the beginning of the universe, this will-power is objectless. It is due to the will of the Lord that the desire to enjoy objects is generated. This results in an unending series of bir hs and deaths. In other words, as Abhinavagupta, the great philosopher and teacher of *KŚ* bluntly puts it :

> God of devas creates the bondage and it is that God Himself who releases him from the bond.[20]

SŚ MALA

This is regarded as Śiva's 'playfulness'! *SŚ* regards this *mala* as great bondage (*mahā-pāśa*). It is not destroyed even in *pralaya* when the whole universe is annihilated. It sticks to the *jīva*. Immediately after the recreation of the new universe, this *pāśa* drags the *jīva* from one birth to another like a beast.[21]

MĀYĪYA MALA

Māyā is a very complex term in Indian philosophy. Great controversies both oral and written have been recorded in many books in India and the West in modern times. But the concept is still elusive. Kaśmir *Śaivas* briefly explain it as "the bond that makes *jīva* to see difference or un-relatedness in himself and other persons and objects (*bhinna-vedya-prathā*). This causes pleasure, pain, transmigration of the Soul. *Siddhānts Śaivas* regarded *māyā* as real, eternal and the material cause of the world.[22] As *māyā* is real, its creation, the world is real. This *māyīya mala* or *pāśa* is accepted in one form or the other by other sects of Śaivism.

Moksa

Mokṣa or liberation from *Saṁsāra* has been the goal of all school of Indian philosophy (except the materialistic school of Bṛhaspati). The concepts of *mokṣa* or *nirvāṇa* are slightly different. Limiting ourselves to Śaivism, *mokṣa* means release from bonds or *pāśas*. With the grace of Śiva, ultimately *āṇava mala* disappears and the *jīvātman* or *paśu* becomes free. Kaśmir Śaivism regards *bandha* and *mokṣa* as mere fiction, as Lord Śiva is present everywhere. The great *KŚ* Ācārya Somānanda, in his work *Śiva-dṛṣṭi* says : As there is no real *bandha*, there is no *mokṣa* to *jīvātman*. This is obviously an echo of Īśvara-Kṛṣṇa's *Sāṅkhya-Kārikā*.[23] To quote Somānanda : "As Lord Śiva is ubiquituous everywhere, there is no real existence to *Bandha* or *Mokṣa* — As there is no real bondage to the Soul there is no stage called 'release' to him due to the non-existence of *Bandha*."[24] In this stage, *jīvātman* becomes **like** Śiva. The Pāśupatas regard *mokṣa* as an end to miseries (*duḥkhānta*). *Siddhānta Śaiva*s regard it as "similarity to Śiva (*Śiva-Sādṛśya*). When all *mala*s are cleansed, Śiva, **out of grace**, gives the *jīva* similarity to Himself. Śrīkaṇṭha, an Ācārya of *Viśiṣṭādvaita* persuasion, in his *BMB* opines that even after parity with Śiva, the liberated Soul has not the higher powers of Śiva such as the creation of the universe and the like.[26]

It is not within the parameters of this work to compare the concept of *mokṣa* in other systems like the Buddhists or Jains. In passing it may be noted that the concept of *mokṣa* in *Śāṅkarādvaita* viz. complete merger of the *jīva* in the *Brahman*, is not accepted even in *KŚ*.

Tattvas (Principles, Categories)

Since ancient times, Man has been trying to understand and decipher the riddle of the universe. Amazed at the vast, unending vista of the world, the seer of the *Nāsadīya Sūkta* in the *Ṛgveda* (*ṚV*, X.129) asks :

> Wherefrom has this Cosmogony come?
> Who is the chief architect?
> Does he know about it?[27]

Dr. R.D. Ranade points out that terms *asat* in this *Sūkta* which is generally translated as 'non-being' is not absolute non-existence but the *archa* of all things. The speculation that *asat* (non-being) is the cause of the universe persisted from Vedic times to the Upaniṣadic period. Thus the *Chāndogya Upaniṣad*. (*Ch. Up.*) states that *sat* was evolved out of *asat*[28] — a view shared by the *Taittirīya Upaniṣad* (*Tait. Up.*). The *Ch.Up.* however accepts the decision in favour of *sat* as the cause of the universe as explained by Āruṇi to Śvetaketu[29] Āruṇi further says that the *sat* entered into its own evolutes (called 'deities' there) viz. (1) Fire, (2) Water and (3) Earth and unfolded both Name and Form (i.e., the entire universe).[30] This entry in three 'deities' or *bhūtas* (elements) is called *trivṛt-karaṇa*. Śaṅkara explains : "In everything there are three *bhūtas*, viz. (1) Fire, (2) Water and (3) Earth. Out of them one element is dominated while the other two elements are in a subordinate position. This *trivṛt-karaṇa* is obviously the precursor of the theory of *Pañcīkaraṇa* of later day *Vedānta* when five elements, earth, water, fire, wind and the ether came to be recognized. The *Chāndogya* concept of *trivṛt-karaṇa* shows a close relationship between microcosm and macrocosm in that ancient period.

The *Sāṅkhya* Theory Anticipated

The *Ch.Up.* goes a step further and attributes colours to these *bhūtas*. Āruni explains to Śvetaketu :

Fire is red, water is white and earth is black.

He emphasizes that what exists is only three colours and the rest is only name and form.[31]

As is well-known, according to *Sāṅkhyas* the colours of three *guṇas* — *sattva*, *rajas* and *tamas* — are respectively white, red and black. *Prakṛti* consists of these three *guṇas*. *Sāṅkhyas*, *Prakṛti* and its evolutes under the wide name "Name and Form" (*nāma-rūpa*) are found in the *Ch. Up.*

SĀṄKHYA ANALYSIS

Important from the point of *Śaiva* (and *Vaiṣṇava*) schools are the twenty-four *tattvas* of *Sāṅkhya* as they are adopted by all these schools. But in between *Upaniṣads* and Classical *Sāṅkhya* is an early *Śāṅkhya* school elaborated by Caraka (AD 78). At one place he states that there are six elements (*dhātus*), viz., the five elements such as earth, water, etc., and *cetana* (Consciousness). Elsewhere he presents another point of view and categories or *tattvas* are said to be twenty-four, viz. ten senses (five cognitive **plus** five conative), *manas* (mind), five objects of senses and then eighfold *prakṛti* viz., *prakṛti*, *mahat ahaṁkāra* and five elements (*bhūtas*). Caraka does not mention *tanmātras*.

Caraka identifies the unmanifest (*avyakta*) part of *prakṛti* with *puruṣa* forming one (*puruṣa-prakṛti*) category — a sort of Śiva-Śakti identity in *Śaivism*. But there is some difference. *Vikāras* or evolutes of *prakṛti* are the *kṣetra* while the *avyakta* part of *prakṛti*, viz. (*puruṣa*) is regarded as *kṣetrajña*.[32] Caraka and Āsuri (the disciple of Pañcaśikha, the great disciple of Kapila) hold similar views in general. Āsuri regards the final state like that of special characteristics (*aliṅga*). The *Mahābhārata* (*Mbh*), *Śāntiparva*, 31.70 ff., mentions three schools of *Sāṅkhyas* admitting respectively twenty-four, twenty-five and twenty-six categories or principles. The *Mbh* recommends the realization of twenty-sixth (*puruṣa*) principle for escape from *saṁsāra*.

A tabular statement of the Principles and their evolutes as given by *Sāṅkhyas* and *Kaśmira Śaivas* and *Siddhānta Śaivas* are given as Appendix I to this chapter.

TATTVAS IN SAIVISM

Śaivism (and Vaiṣṇavism as well) have accepted twenty-four *tattvas of Sāṅkhyas*. They, however, posit twelve *tattvas* above *Sāṅkhya tattvas* and then show how everything has been evolved from Śiva. All schools of Śaivism accept thirtysix *tattvas* in general, though there are some differences in details. These will be discussed separately in the treatment of different schools. A Tabular statement of *tattvas* according to *Siddhānta Śaivism* will show a close similarity in different *Śaiva* schools.

As a specimen of Śaiva analysis of *tattvas*, the analysis of *tattvas* in Kaśmir *Śaivism* is given as follows :

KŚ is a Monist. They have to explain our day-to-day experience of difference and distinction between 'I' and 'This' (the outside world). They have given the gradation of devolution of universal experience as follows:

Stage I : *Śiva*

Śiva and Śakti being identical the experience is "All am I" (*sarvam aham*).

Stage II : *Sadāśiva tattva*

At this stage of manifestation (*ābhāsa*) the experience of 'I'-ness is more dominant than the 'This'-ness (the experience of outside world). The 'I' has a very vague idea of 'This', like that of a painter having a vague outline of a picture he proposes to paint. They call it *anunmīlita-citra-nyāya* Kṣemarāja in *Pratyabhijñā-hṛdaya* (on *sūtra* 3) explains : "(At this stage) experience is dominated (*ācchādita*) by the consciousness of 'I-ness' (*ahantā*) and (the experience of) *Thisness* (*idantā*) is yet incipient (*asphuṭa*)".

Stage III : *The Īśvara Tattva*

The consciousness of 'Thisness' grows viz 'I am this' (*idam-aham vimarśa*). Both consciousness of *I* (*ahantā*) and that of 'this' are simultaneously distinct (*sphuṭa*) — Ksemarāja (*op. cit.*, p 50).

Stage IV : *Śuddha Vidyā*

Here the distinctness of 'I'-ness and 'This-ness' is complete (*aham aham-idam-idam vimarśa*).

These stages do not conceal Śivahood and hence are called "Pure Path" (*suddhādhvan*). The *tattvas* after This viz *māyā* to *niyati* conceal Śivahood and restrict the divine — Śivalike powers of Śiva. As these *tattvas* conceal Śivahood, they are called 'Impure Path' (*aśuddhādhvan*).

The remaining *tattvas* are the same as those of *Sāṅkhyas*. *Siddhānta Śaivism* accepts the reality of *māyā* and of Śiva. Discussion of their *tattvas* will be found in the chapter on Śaiva Dualism in (*Siddhānta Śaivism*).

It will be seen that *tattvas* from (11) *puruṣa* to (36) *pṛthivī* are borrowed from *Sāṅkhyas*. The first *tattvas* (1-5) will be discussed in the section in Kaśmira *Śaivism*.

Liṅga Worship

All Śaiva Sects have prescribed Śiva-worship essential for attaining *mokṣa*. For this worship the *liṅga* as the representive symbol is accepted by all sects.

The history of evolution of the *liṅga* worship is interesting. In this field, the spade of the archaeologist or hypothetical forms with asteriks from the imagination of linguists, are not the proper guides. Theories about Śiva being pre-Vedic or post-Vedic are irrelevent. The fundamental principle of the universe which is both immanent and transcendantal is called Śiva, Viṣṇu or the *Brahman* for the convenience of linguistic expression. It is beyond the scope of such discussion. Persons who have devoted their lives for the realization of that Reality are not at all interested in such fruitless wranglings. Śaivites regard the *liṅga* as the object of worship and meditation for the realization of the highest principle. It is however interesting to know how the *liṅga* worship came to be accepted.

AGNI : RUDRA

The importance of fire in the life of man needs no discussion. It was probably the greatest invention of early man when he could produce fire by attrition. But the trouble of rubbing two pieces of wood was so exhausting that people thought it essential to keep fire unextinguished as the rekindling by attrition was not so easy. Preservation of fire all the twenty-four hours in every homestead was absolutely necessary. It was given a religious bias and maintenance of *Agni-hotra* became essential for every hcuse-holder (*gṛhastha*). The development of simple domestic worship into elaborate sacrifices (*yajñas*), like *Soma*, *Aśvamedha*, *Rājasūya*, etc. was the result of the growing affluence of the society. But fire, the friend of man, was originally a 'roarer' in forest conflagrations and was called *Rudra* (the roarer) even after its 'domestication'. This identification of Rudra and Fire (*agni*) is stated in the *Taittirīya Saṁhitā* (*Tait. S.*) as follows :

"This is verily Rudra that is Fire"[34] and the identity of forest-fire and domestic fire came to be established. Seers of *Rudrādhyāya* (*Tait. S.*, IV.5.7 and of the *Vājasaneyī Saṁhitā* (*VS* chs. 16 and 18), used epithets common to both. Thus in the *Rudrādhyāya*, tawny and reddish brown (*babhru*) reddish (*aruṇa*, *vilohita*), blue or blue-throated (*nīla-grīva*), bluish-red (*nīla-lohita*) : All these are the colours of flames of fire, i.e., of Fire (god). Fire with a smoky crown is Rudra with a mass of hair (*jaṭās*) : in *kaparadin*, smokeless fire is *vyupta-keśa* Rudra (of shaven head).

This identity between Rudra and fire is found even in *ṚV*, I A3.4.[35] The association of Rudra and *agni* in public mind was so powerful that the association of *agni* and *vāyu*, Soma and other deities came to be superseded and forgotten with lapse of time. An additional evidence of the popularity of the identity of Rudra and *agni* is found in the *Atharva Veda* (15.5.1.7) and the *Śatapatha Brāhmaṇa* (1.7.3.8) where the eight epithets of Rudra and *agni* are common.

In *Purāṇas* we are told that gods Brahmā and Viṣṇu advanced against each other to prove their respective superiority. Śiva manifested himself in the form of a column of fire between them and subdued them both, by showing his infiniteness and their inferiority to him. This legend and the identity of the fire blazing in the sacrificial pit (*kuṇḍa*) probably gives a clue to the shape of the *liṅga*.

MUKHA LIṄGAS*

It will be seen that *liṅga* worship is not penis-worship. Śiva-Liṅga is identified with god Rudra, we find the Face(s) of Śiva carved in the *liṅga* since ancient times[36] while human penis is faceless.

LIṄGAS WITH FACES

Śiva is credited to have the following five faces :

Sadyojāta, *Vāmadeva*, *Aghora*, *Tat-Puruṣa* and *Īśāna*. *Śiva-Liṅgas* with five faces are found at Bhita near Allahabad. This belongs to the second century BC. Bhagavan Ekaliṅgajī, the guardian deity of erstwhile state of Mewar (Udaipur), Rajasthan, is a *liṅga* with five faces.

LIṄGAS WITH FOUR FACES

According to the *Mbh. Anuśāsana Parvan*, 140-47 Śiva has the following four faces : *Aghera, Uṣṇīśa* (Turbaned one), *Yogī* and a woman. *Liṅgas* with four faces are found at Bhita, Mathurā and Kauśāmbī (Modern Kosam near Allahabad — both belonging to *circa* 200 BC).

VIGRAHA LIṄGAS

Liṅgas with full form of Śiva inscribed (as if it is the icon of Śiva) are called *Vigraha Liṅgas* (*vigraha* = Body). One such *liṅga* is near Renuguntha (Tamil Nadu). It is famous

---

* The *Liṅgas* which have the faces of Śiva carved on them are *Mukha-Liṅgas*.

as Paraśurāmeśvara. Another *Vigraha Liṅga* is at Gamaru, near Bharatpur (Rajasthan). All these *liṅgas* belong to the Kuśāṇa period. Two more *Vigraha Liṅgas* are in Philadelphia Museum (USA.).

These *Mukha Liṅgas* and *Vigraha Liṅgas* expose the patent mischievous absurdity in equating Śiva Liṅga with Śiva's penis.

STHĀṆU LIṄGAS

Faceless *liṅgas* are called *Sthāṇu Liṅgas*. *Sthāṇu* (a column) form is traced to the legend recorded in different *Purāṇas* like the *Liṅga* (ch. 17), the *Kūrma* (I.26.68-99), the *Vāyu* and others. According to this legend, when gods Brahmā and Viṣṇu began to quarrel about their personal superiority and were on the verge of fighting, a huge column of fire — a *liṅga* of fire — intervened and asserted his superiority over both of them. It was a fiery god Śiva who manifested himself in the *Liṅga* form.

LIṄGA : THE PARA BRAHMAN

The *Śivānubhava Sūtra* (3.3) defines *Liṅga* as follows:

> That in which all mobiles and immobiles enter, i.e., get dissolved, and that from which the universe goes out, i.e., is created, is called a *Liṅga* by those who are experts in the Principle called *Liṅga*.

Thus the word *liṅga* is traced to two Sanskrit roots $\sqrt{l\bar{\imath}}$ — 'to dissolve' and $\sqrt{gam}$ — to go, to get manifested or created. This concept of *liṅga* is similar to the Upaniṣadic concept of the *Brahman* expressed in the *Ch. Up*. as *TAJJALĀN*, Śaṅkara explains this expression as follows:

> *TAJJA* : That form which all elements such as earth, water, fire etc. are evolved.
>
> *TALLA* : That in which the universe is absorbed or dissolved.

and √*an* —'to breathe'—That in which the universe breathes, exists and makes movements (*prāṇiti*). Thus the term *liṅga* means the *Brahman* according to these schools.

It will thus be seen that *Śiva-Liṅga* is the symbol (*liṅga*) of the ultimate Reality which *Śaiva*s designate as *Pati* and *Vedāntin*s as the *Brahman*.

APPENDIX I

Categories or Principles (*Tattvas*) and Their Evolution as per *Sāṅkhyas*

(*Puruṣa* being Aloof is not Included)

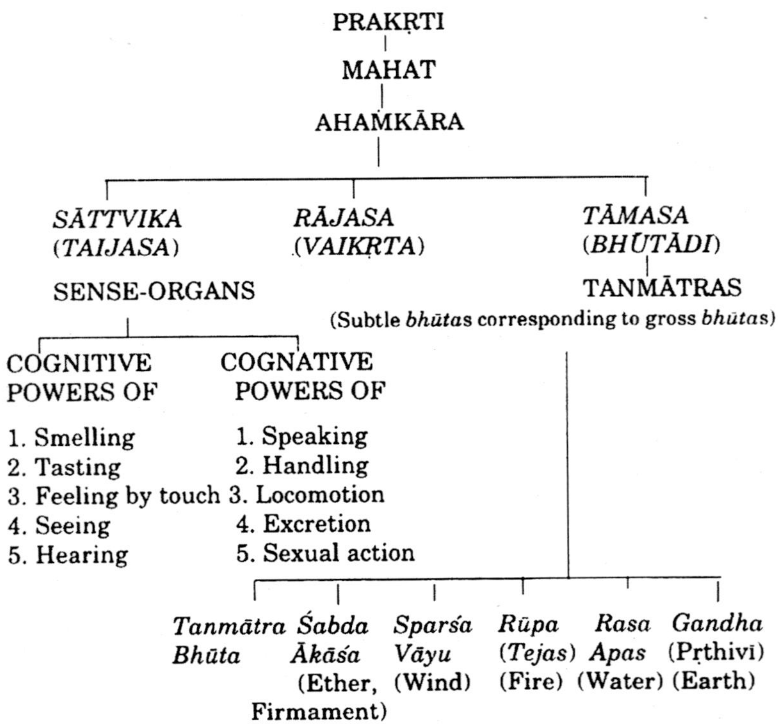

APPENDIX II

Tattvas Analysed (as per Kaśmir Śaivism)

I. *TATTVAS* OF THE UNIVERSEAL EXPERIENCE (1-5)

1. *Śiva* 2. *Śakti* 3. *Sadāśiva or Sādākhya*

4. *Īśvara* 5. *Sadvidyā or Śuddha Vidyā*

II. *TATTVAS* OF THE LIMITED INDIVIDUAL EXPERIENCE (6-11)

6. *Māyā* 7. *Kāla* 8. *Vidyā*

9. *Rāga* 10. *Kalā* 11. *Niyati*

(Tattvas from 7 to 11 both inclusive are regarded as the *kañcukas* of *māyā*).

III. *TATTVAS* OF THE LIMITED INDIVIDUAL (12-13)

12. *Puruṣa* 13. *Prakṛti*

IV. *TATTVAS* OF MENTAL OPERATION (14-16)

14. *Buddhi* 15. *Ahaṁkāra* 16. *Manas*

V. *TATTVAS* OF SENSE EXPERIENCE

The five powers of sense-perception

The power of 17. Smelling, 18. Tasting, 19. Perception or seeing, 20. Tactile or feeling by sense, 21. Audition or hearing.

VI. *KARMENDRIYAS* (CONATIVE ORGANS) : 22-26

Power of 22. Speaking, 23. Handling, 24. Locomotion or moving or walking, 25. Excretion, 26. Sexual action.

VII. *TANMĀTRAS* (SUBTLE *BHUTAS*) : 27-31

27. *Śabda* 28. *Sparśa* 29. *Rūpa*

30. *Rasa* 31. *Gandha*

VIII. *TATTVAS* OF MATERIALITY (FIVE BHŪTAS) : 32-36

32. *Ākāśa* 33. *Vāyu* 34. *Tejas*

35. *Apas* 36. *Pṛthivī*

APPENDIX III

Classification of *Tattvas* According to *Siddhānta Śaivas* (Dualists)

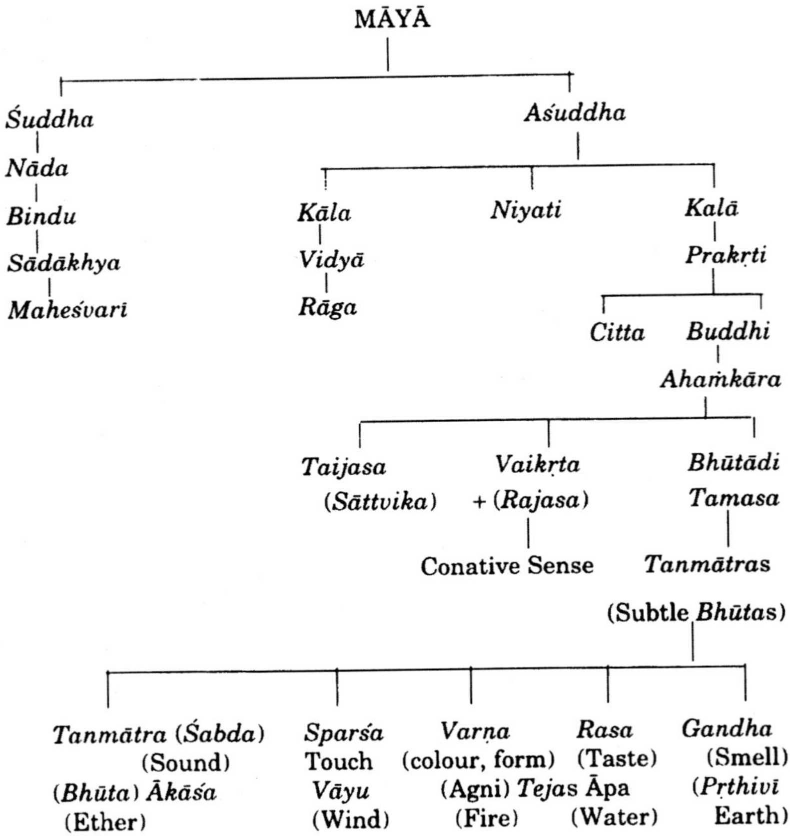

Based on : T.M.P. Mahadevan—*Śaiva Sidhanta. History of Philosophy.*

Notes

1. *āpti, pāti ca paśūn īty ataḥ patir bhavatī* —*Pāś. S.*, p.5.
2. *tasmāt prasādāt sa duḥkhāntam pratiyate* ı

na tu jñāna-vairāgya dharmaiśvarya-tyāga-mātrāt ।

— *Pāś.S.*, p.6.

3. *yam evaiṣa vṛṇute tena labhyaḥ* ।
tasyaiṣa ātmā vivṛṇute tanūm svām

— *Kaṭha Up.*, 1.2.23.

4. (*patiḥ*) *yadi nirvimarśaḥ syāt*
anīśvaraḥ jaḍaśca prasajyeta ।

— *Kṣemarāja* : *Parā Prāveśikā*, p.2.

5. Kṣemarāja, in his commentary on Vasugupta's *Śiva-sūtra*, claims that these *sūtras* were imparted by Śiva in his dream.
dvaita-darśanādhivāsitaprāye jīva-lokerahasya-saṁparadāyo (= *Īśvarādvaya-vāda*) *mā vicehedi ityāśayataḥ* . . . . *parama-śivena svapne'nugṛhya* . . . . *śiva-sūtrāṇi* . . . *sacchiṣyeṣu prakāsitavān*

6. *pumbhyaḥ phalaṁ vicitram dadāti saṁvīkṣya bandha-vaicitryam* ।
svamahimnā nādyudayo nāyatto namo namas tasmai ॥
— Sadyojyoti, *Tattva-traya-nirṇaya* (ed. G.V. Tagare — *Parāmarśa*, Pune University)

7. *śīva-puruṣāvatisānkhau*
prasava-vihīnau citā saṁsthau ।

— *op. cit.*, 2nd verse.

8. *sūkṣma-cid-acid-viśiṣṭam*
brahma kāraṇam, sthūla cid-acid viśiṣṭam kāryam ।

— *BMB*, 1.1.5; 1.27 (I.p.14)

9. *anantānanda-katlyāṇaguṇaika-*
ghana īśvaraḥ śiva ity eva ucyate

— *BMB*, 3.2.17 (vol. II pp.248-49).

10. *janmādi-sṛṣṭi-sthiti-vilaya tirodhanā'nugrahātmakaṁ*
kṛtya-pañcakashyacidacit prapuñca-vilāsasya

— *Śrīkara Bhāṣya*, II, p. 29

Here the words *cit, acit* etc. show the *Viśiṣṭādvaita* characteristic of Vīra-Śaivism.

11. *brahmādyāḥ sthāvarāntāś ca deva-devasya dhīmataḥ* ।
paśavaḥ pari kīrtyante saṁsāra-vaśa-vartinaḥ
teṣām patitvād bhagavān rudraḥ paśupatiḥ smṛtaḥ ।

— *Liṅga Purāṇa* quoted in Bhojadeva's *Tattva-Prakāśa*

12. *ātmā na jāyate* ।
Not only that but he is by nature knowledge itself (*jña*) in *BMB* on *Br. S.*, 2.3.19 viz. *jño' ta eva* Śaṅkara holds similar view.

13. *sāṅkhya-yogena ye muktāḥ sāṅkhya-yogeśvarāś ca ye* ।
brahmādayas tiryagāntāḥ sarve te paśavaḥ smṛtāḥ ॥
— *Pāś. S.*, 31.

14. *puryaṣṭakam antaḥ-karaṇam dhī-karma-karaṇāni* ।
— *Tattva-prakāśa* (*T. Pr.*), 1.12.

15. *BMB* on *Prakāśādivat*
— *Br. S.*, 2.3.24-27

16. *ajñānam kila bandha-hetur iditaḥ* ।
śāstre malam tat smṛtam ।
— Abhinavagupta : *Tantra-Sāra*, p.5

17. *Ajñānam it na jñanābhāvaḥ . . . . sa loṣṭhādike' pyasti*
— *op. cit.*, p. 28

18. *jñanani bandhaḥ* ।
— *Śiva S.*, 1.2.

19. *jñā'nau iti jīvasyā'jñatvam kiñcij-jñatvam eva* ।
— *BMB*, 2.142

20. *svayam badhnāti deveśaḥ svayam eva vimuñcati* ।
— *Tantrāloka*, 8.82

21. *karmākhyo' yam mahā-pāśo durmocas tenajantavaḥ* ।
itas-tataḥ samākṛṣya nīyante paśava iva ॥
— Quoted from the commentary on *T. Pr.*, 1.16

22. (i) *māyā vastūrūpā mūlam viśvasya nityā sā* ।
— *T.Pr.*, 1.18.

(ii) *māyā tāvanna parameśvarādhiṣṭhitā jaḍā, jagad-upādānam bhavati* ।
maheśvaraś cetano'pi na māyām vinā jagad mūlatām bhajate ।
— *op.cit.*, p.62

23. *tasmānna baddhate' ddhā ṇa mucyate, nā'pi santarati kaścit* ।
— Iśvarakṛṣṇa — *Sāṅkhya-Kārikā*, p. 62

24. *bandha-mokṣau na bhidyete sarvatraiva śivatvataḥ* ।
pratīti-mātram evātra tāvataḥ bandha-mokṣatā ।
— *Śiva-dṛṣṭi* 365-69 also 370-72

25. *tasya prasādāt sa duḥkhāntaḥ prāpyate* ।
— *Pāś. S.*, p.6.

26. *muktasya parameśvara-sāmye' pi*
jagat-sṛṣṭyādi vyāpāra-varjam
eva svātantryam asya bhoga-vastuṣu ।
— *BMB*, II.496

27. *iyaṁ visṛṣṭir yata ābabhūva* ।
. . . . jo' syādhyakṣaḥ parame vyoman ।
so'ṅga veda yadi vā na veda ॥
— *ṚV*, X.129

28. *asad eva idam agra āsīt* ।
ekam evādvitīyam ।
tasmād asataḥ saj-jāyata ।
— *Chāndogya Upaniṣad*, 6.2.1

29. *satveva somyedaṁ agra āsīd ekam evādvitīyam*
tad aikṣata 'bahu syām prajāyeya' ।
— *op. cit.*, 6.2. 2-3 ।

30. *hanta, ahaṁ tisro devatā anena*
jīvenātmanā'nu praviśya
nāma-rūpe vyākaravāṇī ।
— *op. cit.*, 6.3.2 and 3

31. *yad-agne rohita, rūpaṁ tejasas tad rūpam, yacchuklam tadapām* ।
yat kṛṣṇaṁ tad annasya pṛthivyāḥ . . . . vācārambhaṇam
vikāro nāmadheyam trīṇi rūpāṇītyeva satyam ।
op. cit., 6.4.1

32. *avyakta-madhyasya kṣetrasya*
kṣetrajñam ṛṣayo viduḥ ।
For details — S.N.Dasgupta, *History of Indian Philosophy* Vol. I, p. 216 ff.

33. *janma-mṛtyu-bhayād bhītā yoga-saṅkhyāśca kaśyapa* ।
sad-viṁśam anupaśyantaḥ śucayas tat-parāyaṇāḥ ।
yadā sa kevalībhūtaḥ ṣaḍviṁśaṁ anupasyati ।
tadā sa sarvavid vidvān punar janma na vindati ।
— *Mbh Śānti*, 318.79-81

34. *rudro vā eṣa tad agniḥ*
— *Taitt. S.*, V. 4.3.1.

35. *gāthapatim medhapatim rudram jalāpabheṣajam* ।
— *ṚV*, 1.43.4 also *AV*, 7.8.7.1
The similarities between the procedure of Fire-worship and Linga-worship are practically the same — G.B. Dandage *Rudra, Yajña and Śive-Liṅga* (Marathi book, Maharashtra Grantha Bhandar, Kolhapur).

36. N.P. Joshi — *Bharatiya Mūrtiśāstra* (Indian Iconography), Marathi, Maharashtra Universities Book Production Board, Nagpur.

37 *līyate gamyate yatra, yena sarvam carācaram* ।
tadeva liṅgam ityuktaṁ liṅga-tattva-parayanaiḥ ॥
— *Śivānubhūti Sūtra*, 3.3

The word *liṅga* is derived from two roots $\sqrt{lī}$ — 'to dissolve', $\sqrt{gam}$ — 'to go'; 'to let out,' 'to create'.

2

Pāśupatism (Dvaitādvaitism)

In the Introduction, we have seen that the term 'School of Śaivism' means the particular relationship between *Pati*, *Paśu* and *Pāśa* adopted or believed by certain thinkers and their followers. This over-simplified concept about the term 'School' is enough for a common reader in the beginning. At first the school called Pāśupatism (*Pāś.*) is considered, as that is the ancient-most and the only *Veda*-based School of Śaivism.

What is Pāśupatism

The term *Pāśupata* means 'pertaining to Paśupati'. *Paśūpati* is 'The Lord of *Paśus*' (bound or enchained *jīvas*). In Vedic literature, *Paśupati* or *Paśūnām patiḥ* is the name of Śiva (*Taitt. Saṁ.*, 4.5.2.1 *Vāj. Saṁ.* chs. 16,17; *Maitrāyaṇī Saṃ.*, 2.9.3) and obeisance is paid to him. The *Āśvalāyana Gṛhya Sūtra* (2.2) specifically mentions that Śiva, Paśupati and Śaṅkara are the names of the same deity.[1]

The *Rudrādhyāya* of *Taitt. Saṁ.* (IV.5 and 7) *Śatarudriya* in *Vāj. Saṁ.* (chs. 16, 18) show that Śiva-worship in some form was in vogue in those times. The *mantras* in *Taitt. Āraṇyaka* (XVII.1-5) were adopted by Lakulīśa, the founder of Pāśupatism, as the basis of his philosophy and *Sādhanā*. But an earlier form of Pāśupatism is traceable to the *Śvetāśvatara Upaniṣad* (*Śv. Up.*). For example : According to *Śv.Up.*, Śiva is the only God and one. He creates the heaven and the earth and pervades it all.[2] But the monotheism of Lakulīśa is more fervid in devotion. He prohibits the worship of gods other than Śiva and of ancestors viz. performance of *śrāddha* on the ground that Śiva is immanent in them.[3] Kauṇḍinya the commentator of *Paś. S.* explains the **rationale** of this instruction. The concept of god Rudra in *Śv. Up.* and *Pati* in *Pāśupata Sūtra* (*Pāś. S.*) is similare to that in *Śv. Up.* It regards Him as the creator, sustainer and annihilator of the universe (*Śv. Up.*, 4.9; 1.8; 5.3). Śiva according to *Śv.Up.* (1.16) is both immanent and transcendant.[4]

The path of *Yoga* seems to be common to both *Śv. Up.* and *Paśu. S.* The *Śv.Up.* states :

One's own body is (the lower) *araṇi* and *praṇava* (*oṁkāra*) is the (upper) *araṇi*, *dhyāna* (meditation) is the attrition (rubbing against) each other. Thus one should see the Lord unmanifest[5] (like an unmanifest spark emanates while rubbing).

The *Śv.Up.* is earlier than the *Bhagavad Gītā* (*BG*) so *Śv.Up.* is definitely earlier than Lakulīśa. I believe that this is enough to show the Vedic roots of Pāsupatism.

Lakuliśa — His Time — Spread of Pāśupatism

THE FOUNDER LAKULĪŚA : HISTORICITY AND TIME

The historical founder of Pāśupatism is Lakulīśa. He is probably called so as his icons all over India show him as holding a wooden staff (*lakuṭa* > *lakula* 'a staff') and an erect position of his penis — a symbol of his being *ūrdhva-retas* (of sublimated sex). *Purāṇa*s like the *Kūrma* (I.53), *Śiva-Vāyavīya Saṁhitā* (2.95) state that he was the 28th incarnation of Śiva and he had four disciples viz., Kuśika, Gārgya, Kauruṣa and Maitra. All these five persons are mentioned in old epigraphs — a proof of their historicity. Lakulīśa was born at Kārwān in Dabhoi Tehsil of Baroda

District, Gujarat. Then he proceeded to Ujjain, Madhya Pradesh.

SPREAD OF PĀŚUPATISM

As to Lakulīśa's time, R.G. Bhandarkar's conjecture (200 BC) is nearer the mark. Rāśikara Kauṇḍinya, the commentator of *Pāśupata Sūtras* belonged to *circa* AD 350. Rājaśekhara Sūri, the Jain commentator of Haribhadra Sūri's *Ṣaḍ-darśana Samuccaya* states that Rāśikara Kauṇḍinya was the 18th teacher from Lakulīśa. A generation is regarded as a period of twenty-five to thirty years. Taking the lower figure, Lakulīśa is 450 (25 × 18) years earlier than Kauṇḍinya. Thus Lakuliśa should be located in *circa* 100 BC. (AD 350 minus 450 years).

This sect spread all over India. The Chinese traveller Hiuen-Tsiang (AD 629-45) mentions Jullandhar (Punjab), Ahicchatra (near Ramnagar, Rohil Khand), Malakuta (Tamil Nadu), Malwa, Maheśvar and Khotan as the centres of Pāśupatas (*Po-shu-po-lo*) Śārṅgadeva's Sintra inscription (*Ep. India*, p. 282) adds Lāṭa (Southern Gujarat), Prayāg, Śrīparvata (Andhra Pradesh), Rāmeśwar. Paśupati Shrine in Nepal is said to have been originally established by Cārumatī, the daughter of Aśoka Maurya. K.C., Panigrahi's, *Archeological Remains at Bhubaneshvar* records the icons of Lakulīśa and other remains of the Sect. in Orissa.

THE BASIC TEXT — PĀŚUPATA SUTRAS (PĀŚ. S.)

Lakulīśa explained his system in 168 pithy *sūtras*. Some *sūtras* attributed to him are the parts of the first five *mantras* of *Taitt. Āraṇyaka*,[6] 17.1-5. For example *Tait. Ār.*, 17.1 is :

> *sadyojātam prapadyāmi, sadyojātāya vai namaḥ* ।
> *bhave bhave nātibhave bhajasva māṁ, bhavodbhāvāya namaḥ* ॥

Lakulīśa composed the following five *sūtras* based on the above *mantra* :

(1) *sadyojātam prapadyāmi* ।

(2) *sadyojātāya vai namaḥ* ।

(3) *bhave bhave nāti bhave* ।

(4) *bhajasva mām* ।

(5) *bhavodbhavāya nahah* ।

— *Pāś. S.*, 1-40-44

It is creditable that Kauṇḍinya created a philosophical school on the basis of these *sūtras*.

It is interesting to note that Sāyaṇa, the commentator of *Ṛgveda* who was interested in textual interpretation and not into its philosophical significance, regards that the *prātikas* (first words) of the first five *mantras* of *Tait. Ār.*, 17 viz. *sadyojāta* (17.1), *vāmadeva* (17.2), *aghora* (17.3), *tat-puruṣa* and *īśāna* (17.5) are the names of the five faces of Śiva and other epithets in those *mantras* such as *śreṣṭha*, *kāla*, *kalavikaraṇa* are Śiva's powers.

Chronologically Kauṇḍinya was more near to Lakulīśa and belonged to his school. We may presume that he understood Lakulīśa's *sūtras* better. Kauṇḍinya does not refer to Jainism, Buddhism, *Vedānta* or *Māyā-Vāda*.

Main Tenets of Pāśupatism

Kauṇḍinya summarises the main tenets of Pāśupatism as follows :

MOKṢA (LIBERATION FROM SAṀSĀRA)

1. *Mokṣa* is not a mere negative state of painlessness. Nor it is complete absorption of the Individual Soul in the Supreme *Brahman* as believed by *Advaitins* of Śaṅkara school. According to *Pāśupatas*, the Individual soul retains

his separateness or independent individuality in the *mokṣa* stage. He is endowed with powers of vision and action (*dṛk-śakti* and *kriyā-śakti*) like that of Maheśvara and enjoys vicinity (*sāmīpya*) near the Lord. All this implies a state of painlessness.

2. There is no mention of a place like Kailāsa as the spatial location of *mokṣa*.

3. Man gets the fruit of his action. But this is not *niyati-vāda*. God through His Grace can and does destroy the effect of *mala* or the *karmans*.

4. *Mokṣa* depends more on the grace of the Lord rather than through human endeavour. This is an echo of *Kaṭha Upaniṣad* (2.23) and *Muṇḍaka Upaniṣad* (3.2.3.)

But God does not behave arbitrarily. He does not revert a liberated soul to *saṁsāra*.

5. There is no trace of *saguṇa bhakti*.

6. Thorough belief and total emphasis on the *japa* of *oṁkāra*. Lakulīśa lays down "One should meditate on Oṁkāra" (*Pāś.*, 5.5.24).[8] Kauṇḍinya explains : "Only Oṁkāra should be meditated upon, not anyone else". Bhāsarvajña, another authority on Pāśupatism, in his commentary on its *Gaṇa-Kārikā* (a standard work on Pāśupatism) "Oṁkāra is the only object worth meditating for (as the cause of) the end of *duḥkha* i.e. *Mokṣa*".

Philosophical Tenets of Pāśupatism Compared With Other Systems

Mādhava, in *Sarva-darśana-Saṅgraha* gives an excellent summary of the Tenets of Pāśupatism, comparing them with those of other schools.

MOKṢA

Other schools (like *Sāṅkhya* and *Yoga*) regard the end of misery (*duḥkhānta*) as *mokṣa*, but in addition to the end of misery, Pāśupatas believe in endowment of the powers (of knowledge and action) of the Supreme soul in the *mokṣa* stage.[9]

KĀRYA (EFFECT)[10]

In other schools *kārya* (effect) has no previous existence. It follows the cause (*kāraṇa*). But *Pāś. S.* says the effects such as *Paśus* (Bound Souls) are eternal (beginningless and endless).

CAUSAL RELATION[11]

In other schools, the Causal relation, the result depending on related cause and *vice versa*. But in Pāśupatism, Maheśvara or *Pati* is the only cause. He does not depend on or gets modified as per effect.

KAIVALYA (MOKṢA)[12]

In other schools, *kaivalya* (aloneness?) implies complete freedom of the Soul from *Prakṛti*. It is the fruit of *yogī*'s efforts. But *Pāśupata Yoga* itself confers Supreme Powers and end of misery.

DIFFERENCE FROM PŪRVA MĪMĀṀSĀ[13]

Other schools (e.g. *Pūrva Mīmāṁsā*) confer fruits like stay in heaven but they result in the re-birth in *Saṁsāra*. In Pāśupatism *mokṣa* is non-return to *saṁsāra* and stay in the vicinity of Maheśvara is the fruit.

Pathway to Liberation

Pāśupatism is no arm-chair philosophy. It has laid down its special path to *mokṣa*. The *sādhanā* starts with renunciation of household *saṁsāra*. It consists of the following five stages in the *sādhanā mārga* of Pāśupatas whereby one attains the *summum bonum*.

STAGE I

The aspirant (*sādhaka*) has to stay in a Śiva temple and perform *bhasma-snāna* (smearing the whole body with holy ashes). He has to wear the *nirmālya* (stale flowers thrown away after Śiva's worship). He is to imitate the loud laugh (*aṭṭahāsa*) of Śiva. He is to perform continuously the *japa* of the *mantra*; *sadyojātam prapadyāmi* etc. (*Tait. Ār.*, 17.1)

STAGE II

Austere penance with strict observance of Yama and Niyama. No god other than Śiva to be worshipped. No performance of *srāddha*. Unswerving devotion to Śiva. Continuous *japa* of the *mantra* : *vāmadevāya namo* etc. (17.2).

STAGE III

To shed off one's ego or self-esteem and pose to behave in such a manner outwardly as will incur censure and insults from the public. Inwardly the *sādhaka* must be pure, self controlled and reasonable, but you have to behave like a mad person or a debauchere ogling and showing amorous gestures to other women as god Śiva did to the wives of sages in the Dāruka Vana. In this stage he is to perform continuously the *japa* of the *mantra*: *aghorebhyo'tha ghorebhyaḥ* (*Tait.Ār.*, 17.3). The rationale of such behaviour is that one reduces one's sins and effects of past *karman* when one is thus censured though one is innocent.

STAGE IV

In order to conceal one's penance etc. the *sādhaka* behaves like a mad or mentally retarded person. He is to stay in a deserted house or hut or in a solitary cave and perform the *japa* of the *mantra* : *tatpuruṣāya vidamahe*. (*Tait. Ār.*, 17.4).

STAGE V

In this last stage, a *Pāśupata yogī* is to stay under a tree in a cemetary or burning place of the dead or under the sky and perform the *japa* of the *mantra* : *īśānaḥ sarva-bhūtānām.* (*Tait. Ār.*, 17.5)

Here one is reminded of the XV *saya* of the *Bhagavatī Sūtra* of Śvetāmbara Jains in which the Ājīvaka Tīrthaṅkara, a senior contemporary of Mahāvīra, named 'Maṅkhali Gosāla' is reported to have behaved in a censurable way as prescribed for the *Pāśupata yogins.* Such behaviour was a part of the *sādhanā* of Ājīvakas. In the *Sarabhaṅga Jātaka* (*Jātaka Tales*, V.12.5). We are told that the third spiritual predecessor of Maṅkhalī Gosāla, the Ājīvaka Tīrthaṅkara called Kisavaccha, incurred censure from the public of Kuṁbhavatī, the capital city of King Daṇḍakin so much so that people spat on him. But when he died eminent ascetics attended his funeral and gods showered down flowers on his body.

Pāśupata was regarded as a Vedic Sect and Ājīvaka as non-Vedic. It appears that both followed similar pathway to liberation. Philosophically Pāśupatism seems to follow *Dvaitāadvaita* (difference-cum-non-difference). The *Āgama* or the path of Lakulīśa was later followed by the ignorantly designated Kālāmukha sect in the eleventh and twelfth century. *Epigraphica Carnatica* records a number of inscriptions from Bijapur and shimoga Districts of Karnataka. These were brāhmaṇas probably migrants from Kaśmir. They were *liṅga*-worshippers and they built *liṅga*-Temples like Kedārevara, Somnāth. Like Pāśupatas they taught *Yoga*, *Śāstra*s etc. to all people as such *vidyādāna* is specifically mentioned in some inscriptions (David N. Lorenzen : *The Kāpālikas and Kālāmukhas*, pp. 97-172). As S.C. Nandimath notes in his *Handbook of Vāraśaivism* these temples are now with Vīraśaivas who follow the tradition of *vidyādāna* : "Slowly and imperceptibly they have been absorbed in Vīraśaivism". *Mysore Gazetteer*

(II part 885) specifically states : "The Saivite revival under Basava — The natural result of the work of those Saiva teachers of the Pāśupata (read for 'Kālāmukha') school of Belagami (= Belagave). It may not be far from truth if one says that though the old Pāśupata school in its pristine purity is not seen today, it has, to some extent, survived in a transformed from — Vīraśaivism".

Notes

1. *paśupataye, śivāya, śaṅkarāya . . . . svāhā* ।
   — *Āśvalāyana Gr. S.*, 2.2
2. *devaḥ ekaḥ samāvṛṇoti* — *Śv. Up.*, 6. 10
   dyāvā-bhūmī janayan deva ekaḥ — *Śv. Up.*, 3.3
3. *deva-vat pitṛvacca* ।
   ubhayam tu rudre devāḥ pitaraśca ।
   — *Pāś. S.*, 2-10-11.
4. *sarva-bhūta-guhāśayaḥ* ।
   sarva-vyāpī bhagavān ।
   — *Śv. Up.*, 1-16
5. *sva-deham araṇim kṛtvā praṇavaṁ co'ttarāraṇim* ।
   dhyāna-nirmathanā bhyāsāt devam paśyet niguḍhavat ॥
   — *Sv. Up*, 1.14.
6. For the convenience of reference those five *mantras* are quoted below :

   17.1 *sadyo-jātaṁ prapadyāmi, sadyojātāya vai namaḥ* ।
   bhave bhave nātibhave bhajasva mām, bhavodbhavāya namaḥ ॥

   17.2 *vāmadevāya namo, jyeṣṭhāya namaḥ, śreṣṭhāya namo, rudrāya namaḥ* ।
   kālāya namaḥ, kalavikaraṇāya namo, balavikaraṇāya namo,
   balapramathanāya namaḥ, sarva bhūtadamanāya namo manonmanāya namaḥ ।

   17.3 *aghorebhyo'tha ghorebhyo ghora-ghoratarebhyaḥ* ।
   saravataḥ sarva-sarvebhyo namaste astu rudra-rūpebyaḥ ॥

   17.4 *tatpuruṣāya vidmahe mahādevāya dhīmahi* ।
   tanno rudraḥ pracodayāt ॥

   17.5 *īśānaḥ sarva-vidyānām iśvaraḥ sarva-bhūtānām* ।
   brahmādhipatir Brahmano'dhipatir brahmā sivo me astu ॥

7. *tasmāt prasādāt sa duḥkhāntaḥ prāpyate* ı
na tu jñana-vairāgya-dharmaīśvarya-tyāgamātrāt ity artha ı
8. The quotations on *Pās. S.*, 5.24 may be grouped as follows :
oṁkāram abhīdhyāyīta (*Pāś. S.*, 5.24)
oṁkāra eva dhyeyo nā'nyaḥ — Kauṇḍinya
duḥkhānta-nimitta-dhyānaika-viṣayatvam oṁkāratvam ı
— Bhāsarvajña in *Ratna Ṭīkā*
9. *anyatra duḥkha-nivṛttir eva dukhāntaḥ* ı
iha tu pāramaiśvarya-prāptiś ca ı
10. *nityam kāryam* ı *kāraneśvara-nityatvat* — *Pāś.S.*
Mādhava explains :
anyatra abhūtva bhāvi kāryam ı
iha tu nityam paśvādi ı
11. *anyatra sāpekṣyaṅ kāraṇam* ı
iha tu nirapekṣah bhagavān eva ı
12. *anyatre karvalyādi-phalakaḥ yogaḥ* ı
iha tu pāramaiśvarya-duḥkhānta-phalakaḥ ı
13. *anyatra punarāvṛttirūpa-svargādi-phalako vidhiḥ* ı
iha punar apunarāvṛttirūpa-sāmīpyādi-phalakaḥ ı
— *Sarva-darśana-Saṅgraha*, p. 75

3

Kaśmir Śaivism

The geographical term 'Kaśmir Śaivism' is wide as four Śaivite sects flourished in Kaśmir. Out of them one was Dualist (*dvaitī*) and was perhaps older and more predominant than the Monist sects as noted by Kṣemarāja, a commentator of Vasugupta's *Śiva-Sūtra*.[1] In *circa* ninth century AD *Ugra-Jyoti* and *Sadyojyoti* were famous teachers of Śaiva Dualism called *Śaiva Siddhānta* a term by which it is now known in Tamil Nadu.

As Aurel Stein notes in the introduction to Kalhaṇa's *Rājataraṅginī* (p.9) Kaśmirīs are a tolerant people as "Buddhism and the orthodox creeds existed peacefully side by side in Kashmir" and the founders of Buddhist *stūpa*s and *vihāra*s "with equal zeal endowed also the shrines of Śiva and Viṣṇu". No struggle between Dualist and Monist Śaivas is recorded.

There were three Monist sects : one propagated by Vasugupta, known as *Trika Śāstra* here. The second is the Kaula system of *Śaiva Yog*a. B.N. Pandit states that the present-day Kaulas of Kaśmir believe that one Maheśvarānanda was their ancestor who came from Mahārāṣṭra and settled in Kaśmir (*Aspects of Kashmir Śaivism,* p. 27). Abhinavagupta belonged to the *śiṣya-paraṁparā* (tradition of disciples) of Vasugupta. But B.N. Pandit states : "Abhinava Gupta's teacher's (Śaṁbhu Nātha's) teacher and grand teacher viz. Soma Nātha and

Sumati Nātha were southerners (*op. cit.*, p. 30) and he supports his statement by quoting a commentary on *Tantrāloka*.[2] The matter needs further investigation as little trace of *Kaula-mata* is found in Mahārāṣṭra.

The third Monistic Śaiva system is the *krama* system. But firstly it is a *Tāntrika* system. Secondly it is a monistic Śaiva system. Thirdly it marks the emergence of the *Śākta* tendency in the Śaiva philosophy. As Navjivan Rastogi puts it, "It (the Krama system) developed into a synthetic and complex whole in which the Śaiva philosophy, the Śākta esotericism and the Tantric synoptic view of life are inter-knitted together" (*The Krama Tantricism of Kashmir Vol. I,* Preface, p. x).

Here we restrict ourselves to the first monistic school of Vasugupta as it is popularly and generally accepted as 'the Kashmir Śaivism'.

This school (and the other two schools) are based on *Āgamas* as contrasted with Pāśupatism which is Vedic. Due to their emphasis on three *tattvas*, *Pati, Paśu* and *Pāśa*, this school is popularly known as *trika* system. Though Āgamic, the followers of these schools call themselves superior to other systems. The gradation of Superiority is claimed as follows[3] : "Śaiva school is superior to the Vedic school". The Superiority grows on as follows : Śaiva . . . . Vāma . . . . Dakṣa . . . Kula (Kaula). "But the Trika is the best of all". (*Trikaṁ Sarvottamam param*). *Parā-Triṁśikā Vivaraṇa*, p.92.

Though *Īśvara-Pratyabhijñā-Vimarśinī* claims that this Sect is open to all : (*yasya kasyacit jantoriti nātra jātyādi apekṣā kācit*), the necessity of Vedic *saṁskāras* shows that it is open only to three *varṇas*.

The influence of orthodox Hinduism was so great that before being initiated into Śaivism, all Vedic *saṁskāras* from Inception (*garbhādhāna*) to marriage must be performed.[4]

Trika-Śāstra

The Kaśmir Śaivism is taken here to imply *Trika Śāstra*. It may be roughly divided as (1) *Āgama Śāstra*, (2) *Spanda Śāstra* and (3) *Pratryabhijñā Śāstra*. J.C. Chatterji points out in *Kashmir Śaivism* (p.7, fn. 1) : "The term Śāstra as employed in this connection does not mean a separate system of thought or treatises dealing with a particular aspect or aspects of the same system". By *śāstra* they imply 'a book'.

Trika-Śaiva Literature

The vast *Trika-Śaiva* Literature may be broadly classified into three divisions : (1) *Āgama Śāstra*, (2) *Spanda Śāstra* and (3) *Pratya-bhijñā Śāstra*.

ĀGAMA ŚĀSTRA

Lord Śiva is the author of the *Āgamas*. Hence they are authoritative like the *Vedas*. Their number is sixtyfour — a number recorded by Śaṅkara in the *Saundarya Laharī* (K.C. Pande in his work on *Abhinavagupta* records the titles of these *Tantras* at pp. 77-80).

About these monistic *Āgamas*, J.C. Chatterji says that though some *Āgamas* are Dualistic, the commentators have striven hard to show them as monistic (*Kashmir Śaivism, op. cit.*, p.9). For example the text of *Mālinī-Vijaya-Tantra* teaches plain, unvarnished dualism but the commentator has shown it to be monistic. Similar monistic interpretation (by commentators) is found in the case of Dualistic *Tantras* like *Svacchanda, Netra, Mātaṅga Tantras* (J.C. Chatterji, *op. cit.*, pp. 9-10) Vasugupta (AD 825) has the credit of bringing out a real monistic system out of such a chaotic state. His work is not polemical like the *Brahma Sūtra* but it explains paths to *mokṣa*. There are four commentaries on the *Śiva Sūtra*. Though I have included them all in my Marathi translation of the *Śiva Sūtra*, here

I have mainly followed Kṣemarāja's commentary, the best one in the lot.

SPANDA ŚĀSTRA

Spanda is 'vibration', 'an apparent movement' but here it is used in the sense of 'The Divine Creative Pulsation'. These *Kārikās* elaborate the principles of the *Śiva Sūtra*. There are a number of commentaries on these *Kārikās* e.g. *Spanda Vṛtti* by Kallaṭa, *Vivṛtti* by Rāma Kaṇṭha, *Spanda-nirṇaya* by Kṣemarāja. I have rendered the *Spanda-Kārikās* (with comm.) in Marathi.

PRATYABHIJÑĀ

The Individual Self or *jīvātman* is Śiva but forgetting his divine nature identifies himself with his psychophysical mechanism called *śarīra* or body. The recognition that 'I am God or Śiva' is *pratyabhijñā*[5]. It is polemic and interprets logically the main doctrines of the system. Hence it is called *manana śāstra* or *vicāra śāstra*.

Somānanda, a disciple of Vasugupta wrote a polemical work of 700 verses called *Śiva-dṛṣṭi*. (Here *dṛṣṭi* means *darśana*, school of philosophy). In his work Somānanda criticises the *Śabda-Brahma-Vāda* of grammarians (2nd *Āhnika*), Śāktism and Śaiva Dualism (3rd *Āhnika*), *Vijñāna-Vāda* of Buddhists (5th *Āhnika*), other *dārśanika* views (6th *Āhnika*) and established Vasugupta's theory of *Īśvarādvaya-Vāda*. As Somānanda was the first polemic writer of the school, Abhinavagupta glorifies him by calling him *Svātmeśvara-pratyabhidhāna-parasya tarkasya kartā*.

A galaxy of Kaśmirian scholars like Utpala, Abhinava-gupta, Kṣemarāja, Jayaratha and others wrote authoritative works on this.

Trika Philosophy

As stated already, Vasugupta's school, is called *Trika*, the triad being *Pati*, *Paśu* and *Pāśa*. The concept of *Pati* in

Trika Śaivism and in other schools is discussed from a comparative point of view in the chapter 1 (*Some Fundamental Concepts*). Here a few more characteristics are noted.

According to *Trika* Śaivism, *pati*, the Ultimate Principle, is *Para Śiva*. Its other designations are : *cit*, *citi*, *parā saṁvit* (The ultimate knowledge) *Parameśvara* (The Supreme Lord or sovereign God etc.). The English renderings are inadequate. For example, *cit* or *citi* is translated as 'Consciousness' — a word implying subject-object relation, a duality. But *cit* is non-relational. It means it has **immediacy** of feeling where **I** and **This** (World, other than 'I') are indistinguishable.

As *Pratyabhijñā-hṛdaya* (*Sūtra* 3, p.54) states :

> It is both immanent and transcendent to the Universe. The universe is God's manifestation *within* Himself. Out of all the (36) *Tattvas* (Principles, categories) *Tattva* from Śiva to *Pṛthvī* is within Him. He is luminous and illuminating and full of Bliss.[6]

Para-Śiva is endowed with *prakāśa* (knowledge). As *Kaṭhopaniṣad* puts it : It shining, everything else is illuminated.[7] In addition to *prakāśa*, *Śiva* has *vimaraśa*, the power to create, destroy or do anything without depending on any outside agency, by sheer will-power. On this point Śiva appears more powerful that Śaṅkarite *Brahman* which cannot create unless it is united with *avidyā*. Kṣemarāja says : If Śiva be *vimarśa*-less he would be powerless and inert.[8] *Vimarśa* or *śakti* is an inalienable integral part of Śiva. To state briefly, Śiva is Śakti, Śakti is Śiva. As Somānanda, the first polemic Ācārya of *Trika* Śaivism says in his *dārśanika* work *Śiva-dṛṣṭi* (3.23) : "Never has Śiva been bereft of *śakti* and *vice-versa*. Śaivas do not recognize any difference between Power (*śakti*) and the possessor of (one endowed with) Power (*śakti*).[9]

Kālidāsa seems to have anticipated this relation between Śiva and Śakti (Pārvatī) when he compares their oneness 'as between word and its meaning' (*Vagarthāviva Samprktau*). Infinite are the powers of Śiva. But Abhinavagupta mentions the following as more prominent:

(1) *cit*, (2) *ānanda*, (3) *icchā*, (4) *jñāna* and (5) *kriyā*.

He succinctly explained them as follows (in *Tantra Sāra*, I. 6) :

(1) *Cit* — Power of self-revelation, of being Light (*prakāśa-rūpatā*)

(2) *Ānanda* — Absolute bliss. It is perfect freedom (*svātantrya*) to do or to be anything.

Cit and *Ānanda* constitute the nature of Śiva.

(3) *Icchā* — Will-power to be anything (*tathā bubhūṣā* or to create anything without obstacles. (*svātantryam-nāma yatheccham tatra icchā - prasarasya avighātaḥ* Hence God is called *Sadāśiva* or *Sādākhya*.

(4) *Jñāna* — Non-emotional knowledge (*īṣattayā vedyonmukhatā*) about everything. Hence Śiva is called *Īśvara*.

(5) *Kriyā* —Power to create everything from Himself. (*sarva-kārya-yogitvam*). Hence Śiva is known as *Sadvidyā* or *Śuddha vidyā*.

Somānanda, in *Śiva Dṛṣṭi* (I. 44-45) explains :

> Just as a *Yogī* can create anything without any *upādāna* (Material cause) so does Śiva's Will :
>
> *tathā bhagavad-icchaiva tathātvena prakśaśate* ।

Utpaladeva explains *tathātvena* in the above verse :

> *bhagavad-icchā-matreṇeva viśvarūpam saṁpadyate*
> Mere will manifests itself in the form of universe.

This is a special characteristic of Śiva in *Trika* thought.

Functions of Śiva

The following five are the functions of Śiva :

(1) *Sṛṣṭi* — √*sṛj* — 'to let go'. The Universe is not created. Śiva uncovers or manifests it.

(2) *Sthiti* — Maintenance of the Universe.

(3) *Saṁhāra* — The process of 'drawing in' (Himself) the Universe which is let out.

(4) *Vilaya* or *Pidhāna* — To cover the real nature of the *jīvātman* (Souls).

(5) *Anugraha* — Grace. There is no *mokṣa* without the grace of Śiva.

The creation, maintenance and destruction of the universe is Śiva's sport (*krīḍā*).

PAŚU (INDIVIDUAL SOUL)

As in other sects of Śaivism, the *Trika* system uses the term *Paśu* for individual souls as they are bound by *Pāśa*s (Bonds) or *mala*s (dirt). The soul is thus encaged in *Puryaṣṭaka* 'a city of eight constituents' viz. the physical apparatus of five *tanmātras* (subtle elements) and the psychic apparatus consisting of intelligence (*buddhi*), Ego or I-ness (*ahaṁkāra*) and Mind (*manas*). This is the *liṅga śarīra* in which the individual soul (*ātma-tattva*) who is really Śiva, is confined, with all his divine Śiva-like powers reduced to an 'atom' (*aṇu*) due to *Pāśa*s or *mala*s. The term *aṇu* does not signify spatial dimension (*pradeśa vyāpti*). The individual soul is transmigrated to another suitable body as decided by his *karma*s.

PĀŚA, BANDHA OR MALA

The topic of *Pāśa* or *bandha* (bondage) or *mala* (dirt) and the three varieties of *Pāśa*, viz *āṇava* (caused by or due to the atom-like power of the individual Soul), *kārmika* or *kārma* (caused by *karmas* or actions of the *jīva*) and *māyīya* (caused by *māyā*) have been adequately discussed in chapter 1. The *Trika* point of view may be summarized here.

Ignorance is the limiting factor of the soul and it (Ignorance) is called *mala* or *Pāśa*. But this Ignorance is partial. Its imposition on the Soul is attributed to the sweet will of Śiva. This original ignorance of *aṇu* (Soul) is called *āṇava mala*. It is imposed by Śiva's will in order to restrict the powers of the *jīvātman* and is hence beginningless. It is however in the *mokṣa* stage that this *mala* is completely washed off. It is due to the bondage (*pāśa*) that *jīvātman* though endowed with *caitanya* (consciousness) like Śiva, came to be designated as *Paśu* and Śiva as *Paśu-pati*. This *mala* is different from the *rāga* concept of *Sāṅkhyas*. That is the quality of the *buddhi* which creates attachment.

The *āṇava mala* is in a way the root or cause of *kārma mala* (*mala* caused by *karmas*) and of *māyīya mala* (*mala* caused by *māyā*).

Kārma Mala

Kārma mala is different from *karma saṃskāra*. The *saṁskāras* are the effects of verbal, physical and mental acts committed by a *jīva*. But *kārma mala* is objectless limited will-power of the Soul and its existence depends on the innate ignorance or *āṇava mala*. In the beginning of the universe, this will power is objectless, but it is due to the Will of the Lord that desire for enjoyment is generated resulting in a series of births and deaths (*saṁsāra*).

As Abhinavagupta remarks in *Tantrāloka* (8.82) "God creates the bondage and God releases a *Jīva* from it". This is Śiva's playfulness at the cost of the *jīvas*.

Māyīya Mala

The bondage caused by *māyā* is *māyīya mala*. By the term *māyā*, the *Trika* Śaivas mean "the misconception of the *jīvātman* that his physical body is the real Self or Soul and that it is distinct and different from other objects". (*Bhinna-vedya-prathā*) The fact of the matter is that there is no difference or distinction between I (*aham*) and the world outside (*idam*). This misconception causes pleasure, pain and rebirth (*saṁsāra*).

MOKṢA

As we have seen in the previous chapter, *Trika* Ācāryas deny the existence of bondage and release. *Mokṣa* is nothing but the awareness of the true nature of the Soul.[11] It is the recognition (*pratyabhijñā*) of our true nature or attainment of the original, innate I-Consciousness (*akṛtrima-aham-vimarśaḥ*). It is simplistically stated in Somānanda's *Śiva-dṛṣṭi* (3.70) "Mokṣa is the realization of one's identity with Śiva".[12] The *mokṣa* stage is not merely the end of misery (*duḥkhānta*) but enjoyment of the supreme bliss and powers of Śiva (except the creation of the world).

ANUGRAHA OR ŚAKTI-PĀTA

Apart from the theoretical discussion about the unreality of Bondage (*bandha*) or Liberation (*mokṣa*), it is everyman's experience that *bandha* is a fact of life from which one should exert oneself to free. But as we have seen in chapter 1, since the times of *Upaniṣads*, it is the experience of sages that self-realization cannot be achieved by intellectual efforts, scholarship, disputations. The Divine Grace is essential for it.[13] *Trika* Śaivism also emphasizes the necessity of Divine Grace (*anugraha*) or Descent of Divine Power (*śakti-pāta*) in man. Persons with powerful spiritual *śaṁskāras* of the previous birth derive this *śakti-pāta* without any *sādhanā*. Mere sight of his Guru is enough for *śakti-pāta* and *mokṣa*. Those who are not so advanced, have to approach a Guru for initiation and perform *sādhanā*. This is called *madhyama śakti-pāta*. People who are still less advanced have some moderate (*manda*) *śakti-pāta* and they get some interest in spiritual matter and they progress slowly.

UPĀYA : PATHWAY TO MOKṢA

According to *Trika Śāstra* there are four pathways to *mokṣa* suitable according to the spiritual progress of the *jiva*. They are (1) *Anupāya,* (2) *Śāṁbhava Upāya,* (3) *Śāktopāya* or *Jñānopāya*, (4) *Āṇavopāya* or *Kṛtyopāya* — the last being for the least advanced persons.

Anupāya

Here *an* means *īṣat* (slight or nominal). A *jīva* whose spiritual advancement (may be of the previous birth) is great, loses his individual consciousness in Śiva, at the word, touch or even the sight (*darśana*) of Guru or even without that. They are instantly blessed with *sakti-pāta* (Descent of the Power of the Lord) or *anugraha* (Divine Grace) and attain *mokṣa*. As this *upāya* refers to a stage in which one achieves self-realization without any Yogic practice, Vasugupta, the founder of this sect, does not deal with this *upāya* either in his *Śiva-Sūtra* or *Spanda Kārikā*.

Śāṁbhavopāya

This is suitable to spiritually advanced aspirants (*sādhaka*s) as it is psychological, depending on meditation. For attaining "pure I-consciousness" (*akrtrima aham*) one has to eliminate *vikalpa*s or the ideation which differentiates between 'this' and 'that' and to attain the stage of pure consciousness (*cit*). Lord Śiva is all-pervading and hence beyond the petty differences of 'this' and 'that'. To achieve this stage, one should meditate on the five functions of Śiva viz. creation (*sṛṣṭi*), maintenance of the world (*sthiti*), *saṁhāra* (withdrawal of the world within Himself), *vilaya* or *pidhāna* (covering, restriction) and *anugraha* (Divine Grace) and try to realize by meditation that all these very functions go on in his individual Self. As noted in *Pratyabhijñā Sūtra* (11) a *saṁsārin* (a person involved in *saṁsāra*) is deluded and is ignorant of his own (Śiva-like) powers. By meditaion one should realize the identity of his individual Soul with Lord Śiva and try to get that experience of identity progressively.

Ultimately the persistent progress of assimilating experience to the consciousness of the *sādhaka* (experient) leads to adsorption in the Lord. When one experiences that the difference between 'I' or mine-ness and the objective world diminishes gradually, the aspirant (*sādhaka*) enters into a psycho-physical state called *bhairavī mudrā*. 'His (*sādhaka*'s) eyesight becomes steady, unwinking and his attention is absorbed in the soul'.[15]

In this *upāya* no physical exertion is necessary as has been prescribed by Patañjali in his *Yoga Sūtra*.

Śāktopāya, Jñanopāya, Mantropāya

The term *Śākta* here has no relation with *Śākta Saṁpradāya*. Here the emphasises is on *mantra-śakti* (power of *mantras*). Hence the term *sāktopāya*. One has to meditate that "I am Śiva" (*Śiva'ham*) or "I am identical with the universe" (*atmaivedam sarvam*). Such meditation leads to the realization of the 'Supreme-I-consciousness' and the aspirant (*sādhaka*) reaches *vikalpa*-less self-realization.

In this *upāya*, meditation and not the physical activities of *Pātañjala Yoga* is advised.

Āṇavopāya or Kṛtyopāya

This is meant for the beginners. It consists of external (physical) activities such as *japa*, *prāṇāyāma*, *dhyāna* (meditation) for the realization of the inner self. As acts like *japa*, *dhyāna* etc. are used in this path to *mokṣa*, it is also called *kriyāyoga*. It included what is called *nādānusādhanā* (concentration on the *japa* of *so'ham* that continuously goes on while we breathe. The number of breaths within twenty-four hours is expected to be 21,600. Concentration on this *nāda* (*so'ham*) is also recommended.) These Śaiva Ācāryas use technical terms for simple processes. Thus for *sa* they use the term *sṛṣṭi bīja* and for *ha*, *saṁhāra bīja*. It is presumed that the sound of *ha* and *sa* while inhaling and exhaling of breath is the *haṁsa mantra*. It is also called *ajapā gāyatrī*. For 'breath' they use the term *vāha*. This *upāya* corresponds to the main steps of *Pātañjala Yoga*.

Although I have followed the *Śiva Sūtra* in the order of giving the *upāyas*, in practice it is the reverse. That is *Ānavopāya* leads to *Śāktopāya* which in its turn is supposed to lead to *Śāmbhavopāya*.

APPENDIX

A few more notes concerning the *Trika* system are added for clarification in the next chapter.

Tattvas

Kaśmira Śaivas are Monists. They had to explain the process of manifestation of the world from the first principle — Śiva. In the chapter of 'Fundamental Concepts' the first six *tattvas* "of the Universal experience" are explained — the hypothesis being that these *tattvas* do not obscure Śiva-hood and were termed as 'The Pure path' (*śuddhādhvam*).

But the fact of the matter is that 'Śivahood' is concealed or obscured. For this they put forward the hypothesis of '*tattvas* limiting Individual experience'. If numbered in continuation of previous *tattvas*, they are (6) *Māyā*, (7) *Kāla*, (8) *Vidyā*, (9) *Rāga*, (10) *Kalā*, (11) *Niyati*. Of these *Māyā* is dominant and *tattvas* (7) to (11) are her *kañcukas* (bodices, i.e., coverings). As they obscure Śivahood, they are cumulatively called *aśuddhādhvam* (Impure Path). *Māyā* as already explained is (*bhinna-vedya-prathā*). The 'universal experience' is now restricted to the separation of experience of '**I**' and '**This**'. *Māyā* is presumed to draw a veil (*āvaraṇa*) on the Self and makes him forget his universal nature. Now to him '**I**' and '**This**', the world other than '**I**' is distinct and different. The next five *tattvas* (7) to (11) are *māyā*'s products and their functions are to 'cover' the nature of the Soul.

(7) *Kalā* : To reduce drastically the universal power of the Self and reduce it to non-entity

(8) *Vidyā* : To reduce the omniscience of the Soul and limit it to individual level.

(9) *Rāga* : To reduce the *pūrṇatva*, complete satisfaction of the universally conscious Self, and create desire for enjoyment of objects.

(10) *Kāla* : To reduce the continuous, indivisible eternity (*nityatva*) and bring about the limitation of Time as Past, Present and Future.

(11) *Niyati* : The unlimited freedom (*svatantratā*) and pervasivness (*vyāpakatā*) of the Original Self are reduced. He is limited in regard to cause, space and form.*

After the 11th *tattva* — establishment of Duality by *māyā*, the remaining 24 *tattva*s are those of *Sāṅkhyas*. They are however classified as follows :

III. Tattvas of Limited Individuality

(12) *Puruṣa* (13) *Prakṛti*

IV. Tattvas of Mental Operation (14-16)

(14) *Buddhi* (15) *Ahaṁkāra* (16) Manas

V. Tattvas of Sense Experience

The five powers of sense perception : Power of (17) Smelling, (18) Tasting, (19) Perception or seeing, (20) Tactile or feeling by senses, (21) Audition or hearing.

VI. Karmendriyas (conative Organs) Powers of

(22) Speaking, (23) Handling, (24) Locomotion, walking, (25) Excretion and (26) Sexual action.

VII. Tanmātras (Subtle Elements of Bhūtas)

(27) *Śabda*, (28) *Sparśa*, (29) *Rūpa*, (30) *Rasa*, (31) *Gandha*

---

* Summarised from *ṣaṭ-triṁśat-sandoha* esp. verses 8-12. On verse 12 the commentator Rājānaka explains that causality is the effect or function of *niyati*.

VIII. Tattvas of Materiality (Five Elements)

(32) *Ākāśa*, (33) *Vāyu*, (34) *Tejas*, (35) *Āpas*, (36) *Pṛthivī*

But elements from 12-36 are adopted from *Sāṅkhyas* and need not be discussed as they are not special to *Trika* Śaivism.

KŚ holds that this variety of the universe is within the 'heart-seed' of the Lord like the leaves, branches etc. of a Nyaggrodha tree are in its seed.[16] That is how they establish their Monist view.

Svātantrya Vāda

This is no *vāda*. It is the special characteristic of Śiva. His independence in creating, destroying or doing anything at will by sheer Will power — without depending on *māyā* or other agency — is known as *svātantrya* (Independence). This sovereign free-will is *svātantrya* of Śiva.[17]

Ābhāsa Vāda

This term consists of two words : *ā* (= *Iṣat* 'slight') and *bhāsa* 'manifestation' or 'appearance'. The world is a **slight** manifestation of the Divine Being or Lord Śiva. Just as the beautiful coloured plumage of a peacock lies in an undifferentiated state in the plasma of its egg, the variegated universe lies within the Lord. The *KŚ* calls this *mayūrāṇḍa-rasa-nyāya*. *Ābhāsa* is external projection of the universe without any external agency — by mere will power.[17] But the projector and the projection are the same just as sea-water and sea-waves (which are nothing but appearances) are the same. The manifestation or projection of the universe makes no difference in the fullness of the Lord as Śiva and the Universe are identical

Saḍadhvā

It is an esoteric topic. To state simplistically : from the point of *parā śakti* (Supreme Power) the manifestation of the Universe takes place in six forms or ways. Hence it is called (*ṣaḍ-adhvā*), *adhvan* = 'a way'. They may be classified as follows :

Subjective Side	*Objective Side*
Vācaka or *Śabda* or *Varṇādhvā*	*Vācya* or *Artha* or *Kalādhvā*
1. *Varṇa*	*Kalā*

2. *Mantra*	*Tattva*
3. *Pada*	*Bhuvana*

Varṇādhvā is like *pramā* — a resting place of *prameya* (object), *pramāṇa* (means of knowledge) and *pramātā* (Experient). Here *varṇa* does not mean 'a colour' or 'a caste'. *Varṇas* are of two kinds. (1) *māyīya* and (2) non-*māyīya*. The *māyīya varṇas* arise out of non-*māyīya varṇas* which are pure, natural, innumerable. The *vācaka śakti* (Indicative power) of non-*māyīya varṇas* is inherent in *māyika varṇas* as the power of hearing.

There is a polarisation between *varṇa* and *kalā*.

There are five *kalās* : (1) *nivṛtti kalā*, (2) *pratiṣṭhā kalā*, (3) *vidyā kalā*, (4) *śāntā kalā* (5) *śantātīta kalā*.

(1) *Nivṛtti kalā* consists mainly of the element Earth and according to Abhinavgupta, it has 16 *bhuvanas* (planes of existence). It is encircled on all sides by (2) *pratiṣṭhā* which in turn is encircled by (3) and so on up to (5). There is no *bhuvana* in (5) but only Śiva-Śakti.

Śiva Transcends All Kalās.

Kevalādvaita and Īśvarādvaita

The term — *advaita* — being common to both the names of schools of Śaṅkara and Vasugupta, there is some confusion in lay people about *Kevalādvaita* (Śāṅkarādvaita) and Vasugupta's *Īśvarādvaya-vāda* as *advaya* and *advaita* apparently appear synonymous. But there are fundamental differences on the following points :

(1) The Supreme Power according to *Vedānta* (including Śāṅkarādvaita) is the *Brahman*. *KŚ* regards Śiva as the Supreme-most power. Though later Śaivas like Śivādvaitins and Vīra Śaivas regards Śiva and the *Brahman* as identical, *KŚ* differs. They say *Parama Śiva* has the power of creating, maintaining, or destroying the universe or doing and undoing anything by dint of his sheer Will-power. For Śiva is endowed with both powers of *Prakāśa* (knowledge) and *Vimarśa* (Power or Śakti — an approximate rendering of the term). But the *Brahman* is mere *prakāśa* (knowledge).

*About the *tattvas* and *bhuvanas* see *Pratyabhijñāhṛdayam*, Jaideva Singh, pp. 152-55. The whole topic is esoteric and complicated.

(2) The *Brahman* by itself is inactive. The World is created with *avidyā* associates with the *Brahman* (called *Īśvara* at this stage). Hence they call Brchman *śānta* (a euphemism for 'impotence').

(3) With Śaṅkara the world is created by *avidyā*. Hence it is *mithyā* (unreal) but *KŚ* hold that the world is created by sheer Will Power of Śiva and as Śiva is real, the world created by him is automatically **real**. Reality of the world is a fundamental difference between *KŚ* and Śaṅkara.

(4) According to Śaṅkara *māyā* is unreal (*mithyā*) — a misconstrued term according to anti-Śaṅkara authors. Śaṅkara holds that *māyā* is unreal (*mithyā*) and indescribable (*anirvacanīya*). But *māyā* is real and is one of the powers of Śiva.

(5) Śaṅkara advocates the Upaniṣadic view that the world is nothing but Name and Form (*nāma-rūpa*). But *KŚ* states that the universe itself is Śiva or is illuminated by Śiva and it is *cid-vilāsa*.

(6) According to Śaṅkara *avidyā* is destroyed by *śravaṇa*, *manana* and *nididhyāsana*. But according to *Trika* Śaivism ignorance is *āṇava* or *pauruṣa* and *bauddhika*. The *bauddhika* (of intelligence) can be destroyed by Śāṅkarite ways mentioned above, but *āṇava* ignorance is eliminated by the grace of God.

For this *dīkṣā* from a *guru* is essential.

There are a few other differences but the essential ones are summarised above.

Notes

1. *dvaita-darśanādnivāsita prāye jīvaloke*
   rahasya-sampradāyo mā viccedī ।
2. *kaścid dakśiṇa-bhūmi pīṭha*
   vasati . . . . loke'bhūt sumatiḥ ।
   — Comm. on *Tantrāloka*
3. *vedāc chaivam, tato vāmam, tato dakṣam, tataḥ kulam* ।
   tato matam tataścāpi trikaṁ sarvottamam matam
   — *Parātriṁśika-vivaraṇa*, p. 92.
4. *garbhādhānāditaḥ-kṛtvā yāvad udvāham eva ca* ।

tāvat tu-vaidikaṁ karma paśćāt śaive hyananyabhāk ।
— *Saiva Agam* quoted in *Tantrāloka-viveka*, p. 278.

5. *aham iśvara-eva nānyaḥ, ity evam yaḥ sākṣātkāraḥ sa pratyabhijñeti ucyate . . .*
— M. Abhyaṅkara's *Darśanāṅkura Ṭīkā* on *Sarva-Darśana-saṅgraha*, p. 190

6. *śrīmat parama-śivasya punaḥ*
viśvottīrṇa-viśvātmaka-
paramānandamaya-prakāśaika-
ghanasya evaṁ-vidhameva śivādi-
dharaṇyantam akhilam abhedena eva
sphurati, na tu vastutaḥ anyat kiñcit.
grāhyam grāhakaṁ vā
— *Pratyabhijñā-hṛdaya-sūtra*, 3

7 *tam eva bhāntam anubhati sarvam* ।
tasya bhāsā sarvam idam vibhāti ।
— *Kaṭha Up.*, 5.15; *Śv. Up.*, 6

8. *yadī (śivaḥ) nir-vimarśaḥ*
syāt (saḥ) anīśvar jaḍaś ca prasajyeta
Kṣemarāja — *Parā-prāveśikā*, p.2

9. *na śivaḥ śakti-rahitaḥ na śaktir vyatirekiṇī* ।
śakti-śakti mator bhedaḥ śaivair jātu na varṇyate ॥
— *Śiva-dṛṣṭi*, 3.23.

10. *bandha-mokṣau na bhidyete sarvatraiva śivatvataḥ* ।
pratiti-matram evātra, tāvata bandha-mokṣatā ।
tadātmtatve nāsti bandhaḥ tadābhāvāt na mokṣatā
— *Śiva-dṛṣṭi*, 365-69; 370-72

11. *mokṣo hi nāma naivānyaḥ svarūpa-prathanam hi tat* ।
— *Tantrāloka*, I, p. 192

12. *śivābheda-pratitimātram mokṣaḥ*
tad-apratitis tu bandhaḥ
— Comm. on *Śiva-dṛṣṭi*, 3.70

13. *nāyam ātma pravacanena*
labhyo, na medhayā, na bahunā śrutena
yamaiveṣa vṛṇute tena labhyaḥ ।
— *Kaṭha Upaniṣad* (2.23)
— *Muṇḍaka Upaniṣad* (3.23)

14. *svayaṁ badhnāti devesaḥ*

svayam eva vimuñcati
— *Tantrāloka*, 8.82

15. *antar-lakṣyo bahir dṛṣṭir*
nimiṣonmeṣa-varjitaḥ ।
iyam sā bhairavī mudrā

16. *yathā nyaggrodha-bījasthaḥ śakti-rūpo mahā-drumaḥ* ।
tathā hṛdaya-bījasthaṁ viśvam etac carācaram ॥
— *Parā-trīṁśika*, quoted by Kṣemarāja

17. *svātantryaṁ nāma yatheccham̐*
tatra icchā-prasarasya avighātaḥ
— *Īśvara-pratyabhijñā*, 1.5.13

18. *cidātmaiva hi devo'ntaḥ sthitam icchāvaśād bahiḥ* ।
yogīva nirupādānam arthajātam prakāśayet ॥
— *Īśvara-Pratyabhijñā*, 1.5.7

4

Siddhānta Śaivism

It is believed that the designation *Śaiva Siddhānta* to this school of Śaiva Dualism (or rather Pluralistic Realism) is given by a Kashmirian author Sadyojyoti (9th cent. AD). In his small treatise *Bhoga Kārikā* (v = verse 2), he says that 'the term *Siddhānta* is applied to Śaivism based on twenty-eight *Tantras* like *Kāmikāgama* composed by Śiva'.[1] In this treatise on *Mokṣa-Kārikā* (v.79) based on the *Śaivāgama* called *Ruru Siddhānta*, he states that this *Siddhānta* leads to *bhoga* (worldly pleasures) and *mokṣa* (liberation from *Saṁsāra*).[2] In *Parā-mokṣa-kārikā*, he refutes both *Pāśupatism* and Vasugupta's *Advayavāda*. Bṛhaspati, the author of *Śiva-tanu-Śāstra* is another dualistic writer of that century. But we do not find a systematic treatment of this school in these works. After Vasugupta, the Kantha family, e.g., Rāmakaṇṭha, Nārāyaṇakaṇṭha upheld the banner of Dualism in Kashmir, but they were swamped by Vasugupta's followers from Kallaṭa to Abhinavagupta and others.

It is, however, not known how *SŚ* (Siddhānta Śaivism) reached Tamil Nadu in the sixth century AD, as Tirumūlar's *Tirumandiram* shows an advanced stage of *SŚ*, as compared with Sadyojyoti's treatises,[3] Sekkiḻār's *Periya Purāṇam*

(*PP*) describes the lives of sixtythree canonical saints of *SŚ* who are known as *Nāyanārs* or *Aḍiyārs*.

The Śaivism popularized by these devotees of Śiva was a cosmopolitan creed. Many of these were of Veḷḷāḷ community, some brāhmaṇas, some Ādivāsīs. Ordinary prejudices of castes did not weigh much on the minds of these *Śiva-bhaktas* (devotees of Śiva). High-caste *Śiva-bhaktas* dined with their low-caste comrades, Ādi Śaiva brāhmaṇa Sundarmūrti ate with Sermān Perumal Nāyanār and married a dancing girl; joint association of Appar (a Veḷḷal) and Sambandhar (a brāhmaṇa) is famous.

Even the brāhmaṇas were not expert in their traditional lore. Very few mastered *Śaiva Āgamas*. The rest of them were *Aḍiyārs* or Toṇḍars (*bhaktas*) pure and simple. About them C.V. Narayan Aiyyar writes : "The saints of *PP* were mostly uncultured folk whose outstanding virtue was their intense Bhakti". (*op. cit.* p. 205) About the 'Victories' over Jains, CVS remarks: "The victories won for Śaivism were through miracles and not through philosophical disputations. (*op. cit.* p. 205) The earliest author-saint-Tirumūlar was claimed to be a *yogī* from Mount Kailās who entered the dead body of a Tamilian — a ruse adopted by some saints. (For example, Lakulīśa, the founder of *Pāśupatism*) to prevent inconvenient probe in the past of the teacher concerned. I believe that Tirumūlar was possibly a Tamilian who went to the North (probably to Kashmir) where he studied *Śaiva Siddhānta* and promulgated it in Tamil Nadu by his work *Tirumandiram*.

The legend about the origin of Vasugupta's *Śiva Sūtra* recorded by Kṣemarāja regarding the age-old prevalence of Śaiva Dualism in Kashmir long before the ninth century AD, is supported by Tirumūlar's work *Tirumandiram* in Tamil Nadu.

Tirumandiram[4] (TM)

This is the first exposition of *SŚ* in Tamil Nadu. It consists of nine *Tantras* or chapters with an introduction (Tam = Tamilian *Pāyiram*) and contains 3,000 and odd verses. It deals with the ethical, metaphysical and mythological aspects of *SŚ*. Tirumūlar regards the *Vedas* and *Āgamas* of equal status as both are created by Lord Śiva. The work is a sort of religious miscellany.

The Tirumandiram (Summary)

The following summary of some of the important topics in each *Tantra* (chapter) will give some broad idea about the nature of the *Tirumandiram*.

The First Tantra begins with *Upadesam* (teaching), then it gives instructions on religious matters such as *agnihotra* (fire-worship), *dāna* (religious gifts) etc., ethical topics like *ahiṁsā* (non-violence), celibacy, preserving equanimity of mind, etc.

The Second Tantra narrates in a nutshell, legends about Śiva (from *Purāṇas* and *Itihāsa*, such as Agastya's arrival in the South, manifestation of *liṅga*, Dakṣa's sacrifice, etc. He interprets the destruction of three *puras* (*tripura*) as the removal of three *malas* (*pāśas*, bonds). He enumerates the five functions of Śiva viz. creation, sustenance and withdrawal (annihilation) of the world, concealment (of powers of Śiva), grace (to confer *mokṣa*), *jīvas* (souls) are classified as *vijñāna-kala*, *sakala* and *pralayākala*. It concludes with an appeal to resort to *guru*.

The Third Tantra is a treatise on yoga, as Tirumūlar conceived it. The eight stages (*aṣṭāṅgas*) of *Yoga of Patañjali* are described. But this *Śiva-yoga* is different from *Pātañjala Yoga*. Even the powers (*siddhis*) acquired after the mastery over some stages are different. For example, mastery over *āsana* (posture) the first *aṅga*, secures the grace of Umā and attainment of stay in Amarāvatī (capital of Indra).

Mastery over the stage called *dhyāna* (meditation) confers the power of moving in regions of gods Brahmā,

Viṣṇu, etc. Patañjali does not mention such *siddhis*, after the mastery of these *aṅgas*. Tirumūlar describes the three great *Śiva Yogas* called *Khecarī, Paryaṅka* and *Candra*.

The Fourth Tantra is esoteric. It gives the *Mantra-Śāstra* or *upāsanā* path of Tirumūlar such as *ajapājapa*, *bhairavī mantra*, six *cakras* like *tripura*, *eroḷī cakra*, *navākṣarī cakra* and describes *pūrṇa śakti*.

The Fifth Tantra describes certain Śaiva paths of liberation such as *śuddha*, *aśuddha*, *mārga* and *kaḍum* (i.e., extremely pure). There is the elaboration of the four parts of *Tantras* viz. *caryā*, *kriyā*, *jñāna* and *yoga*. The three auspicious paths of Śiva-realization viz *sakhā-mārga* (propitiation of Śiva as if he were a friend), *satputra-mārga* (path of behaviour of a good son up to Śiva), *dāsa-mārga* (*bhakti-path* regarding oneself as Śiva's humble servant), the four categories of liberation viz. *sālokya* (living in the same region as that of the.Lord), *sāmīpya* (stay in the vicinity of the Lord) *sārūpya* (similarity in the form like that of the Lord) : four types of Divine grace from 'slow' to 'very intensive', criticism (censuring) of other non-Śaiva paths.

The Sixth Tantra is very useful to the common man. It deals with *Śiva-guru-darśana* (view of Śiva as *guru*), the importance of *vairāgya* (detachment), *tapas* (penance) and knowledge. It ends with the description of worthy and unworthy people.

The Seventh Tantra pertains to yoga. It describes six yogic *cakras*, *ṣaḍadhvā* in *SŚ* six types of *liṅgas* viz. *aṇḍa*, *piṇḍa*, *sadāśiva*, *ātmā*, *jñāna*, and Śiva, need of self-control, characteristics of *sadguru* (spiritual preceptor). Then there is a discussion on yoga, different *mudrās*, abtruse discussion on *bindu*, five *ādityas*, *prāṇāyāma*, the five types of *prāṇa* viz *puruṣa, aṇu, jīva, paśu* and *bodha*.

Lastly the *Tantra* appeals to people to follow the true path.

The Eighth Tantra deals with fundamental teachings of *SŚ*, its differences from the tenets of other schools, eleven spiritual stages, the triads of three *pādas* e.g. (*tat-tvam-asi*), *doṣas*, *kāraṇas* and *śūnyas*. Three categories of each of the three stages — being awake, dream-state and (sound) sleep. The significance of *mahāvākyas* such as *tattvamasi*, *aham brahmāsmi*.

The Ninth and the Last Tantra records Tirumūlar's spiritual experiences such as Dance of Śiva, sight of his real self. It concludes with the eulogy of the omnipresent Lord.

The Śaivism of Tirumūlar

A few topics of *SŚ* may be gleaned from *TM* (*Tirumandiram*). There were four forms of Śaivism: *śuddha, aśuddha, mārga*, and *kaḍuṁ śuddha* (very pure) and four *sādhanas*: *caryā, kriyā, yoga* and *jñāna* (the usual four parts of *tantras*). He discusses the four paths (*mārga*) to Śiva-realization viz. *sanmārga*, *sakhā mārga*, *sat-putra mārga* and *dāsa marga*. We find herein the concept of *śakti nipāta* (descent of power) and its 'speed' of descent: *manda* (slow) *mandatara* (slower), *tīvra* (incessant) and *tīvratara* (more incessant).

Tirumūlar emphasizes the importance of *Śiva-bhakti*. He attempts to synthesize *Vedānta* and *Siddhānta* (*Āgama*). When *Vedānta* is re-inforced by practice, it becomes *Vedānta-Siddhānta*. He uses the term *liṅga* in the sense of sign or index and not the globular stone deity worshipped today. The greatest contribution of Tirumūlar is the synthesis of *Vedānta* and *Siddhānta*. It may be summarised as follows:

1. When the *paraguru* instructs the disciple that the Śiva in the *aṇḍa* (universe) is the same as the Śiva in himself, it corresponds to the *mahāvākya* — *tattvamasi* "That art thou".
2. When one sees the *Sadāśiva Liṅga* and receives divine grace it corresponds to the Truth in the *mahāvākya* — *ahaṁ brahmāsmi*.

3. When the *ātma-liṅga* is visualized and when one rests in pure *cit* it is paralleled to the realization of *brahmaivāham*.
4. When the *jñāna-liṅga* is seen, the stage is indicated *prajñānam brahma*.

In the final stage when *Śiva liṅga* is seen, there is the final union of *jīvātman* and *paramātman* and as there is no distinction between the preceptor and the disciple, there is no *mahāvākya*. (*CVN Aiyyar*, p. 280)

The whole matter is esoteric which a spiritual master can explain.

SAMAYĀCĀRYAS

After Tirumular we have four great Tamil saints. Appar (AD 600-81), Saṁbandhar or Tirujñāna Saṁbandhar (AD 644-60), Māṇikkavācakar (AD 660-92) and Sundaramūrti (AD 710-35).[5] By their sweet devotional songs and ideal *Śiva-bhakti*, they are credited to have ousted Buddhism and Jainism from Tamil Nadu and re-established Śaivism. These saints are regarded as the ideal representatives of paths to Śiva-realization viz. *dāsa mārga* or the path of a servant (service to Śiva), *sat-putra mārga* (the path of an affectionate good son), *sakhā-mārga* (the path of a friend) or *sakhya-bhakti* and *sanmārga* or the true path. These paths (*mārgas*) are regarded as corresponding to (1) *caryā*, (2) *kriyā*, (3) *yoga*, and (4) *jñāna* sections in other schools of Śaivism. The influence of these intensely devotional songs is so great that they are called *Tewāram* and are regarded as Tamilian *Vedas*. They are sung even today in Śiva temples.

Appar

Appar was a rich Veḷḷāḷ (name of his community) of South Arcot district in the reign of King Mahendra I of Kanchi. In search of truth, he embraced Jainism first but later he was miraculously saved by Śiva and so he became a Śaiva. Though he was not a brāhmaṇa, he knew *Upaniṣads* and *Purāṇas* as we hear the echoes of Upaniṣadic philosophy in his songs. He was called Appar (Father, Daddie) by Saṁbandhar (b. AD 639) and thenceforth he became well-known as Appar. Appar insisted on the *japa* of five syllabic *mantra* of Śiva : *śivāya namaḥ*.

Curiously enough Tirumūlar, Appar and Saṁbandhar believe that *Para Viṣṇu* and *Para Śiva* are one in reality and believe that in the liberation stage (*Śiva-mukti*) there is no duality between the individual soul and Śiva. At the lower level, the mythological gods Śiva and Viṣṇu worship each other.

The syncretic icon of *Hari-Hara* is the implication of the Purāṇic legend of Śiva's fascination for Mohinī (Viṣṇu). Appar believed that Śaivism is the real path to *mokṣa*. He used to impart the *mantra śivāya namaḥ* for the realization of Śiva who is beyond 'Name and Form'.

Tirujñāna Saṁbandhar (c. AD 644-60)

Saṁbandhar (Samb.) was a junior contemporary of Appar. He was a brāhmaṇa from Shiyālī (Brahmapurī) *PP* (*Periya Purāṇa*) attributes to him a number of miracles such as Śiva, offering him a pearl palanquin (*SP* = *Saṁbandhar Purāṇa,* v. 226) : curing of the ailment of Malava Princess (*SP,* vv. 318 ff) — an incident mentioned by Saṁb. in (v. 441), resuscitating a dead person at his widow's request (*PP Saṁb Purāṇa,* v. 481) — an incident attested by Saṁb. himself (*PP* Saṁb. 564-70).

But the most important miracle relates to his victory over his Jain rivals in the presence of the King of Madurai. To prove the superiority of their religion, Saṁb. and his Jain rival were asked to write on a palm-leaf and those two leaves were consigned to fire. And lo and behold, the fire did not burn Saṁb.'s palm-leaf. Samb. sang the prayer on the leaf to the King (*PP Samb.* v. 345). It should be noted that in these contests with Jains, matters were decided not on the strength of philosophical disputations but on the occurrences of miracles — some of which are attested by Appar.

PP (v. 1253) tells us that when Saṁb. and his wife went to the Śiva temple at Naḷḷūr Perumaṇam, he prayed to the deity: "O God, bless us with death" (v. 3848) and immediately he and his wife got merged in the *jyotiṣ* or brilliance of the deity.

And to this day, that Saṁb.'s song is sung in that Śiva temple at Naḷḷūr Perumaṇam.

Śaivism in Saṁbandhar

Saṁb. believes in two grades of Śiva. The higher form of Śiva is similar to that of Upaniṣadic *Brahman*. The Higher Śiva is formless and beyond the ken of gods Brahmā and Viṣṇu of the lower grade, though lower grade of Trinity of Brahmā, Viṣṇu and Rudra are created by Him. Vaiṣṇavas too believe in two grades of Viṣṇu and the Trinity of lower grade (Brahmā and others) were created by Mahāviṣṇu.

The Higher Śiva is the creator, sustainer and annihilator of the entire universe (v. 296 and v. 3.448). It reminds us of *Taittirīya Upaniṣad*, III.1. The *Māṇḍūkya Upaniṣad*[7] calls the *Brahman* 'quiescent Śiva' beyond the ken of sight, comprehension, etc.,[8] a characteristic of Higher Śiva in Saṁbandhar. He mentions the Purāṇic legend of Śiva manifesting himself as a column of fire to Brahmā and Viṣṇu (v. 148.9).

In Saṁb. there are some clear concepts of *SŚ* Such as mention of three types of *malas* (v. 119-6), the five functions of Śiva viz. creation, sustenance, withdrawal (annihilator of the universe), concealment and grace. But instead of calling them function, he calls them types of Śiva's grace (Tam. *Aruḷ*) (v. 1433).

Saṁbandhar emphasizes the importance of five-syllabled *mantra* (*śivāya namaḥ*) as the esoteric essence of the *Vedas*, the *japa* of which is essential for liberation. Brahmā and Viṣṇu could visualize the fire-column form of Śiva due to the *japa* of this *mantra*. Saṁbandhar advises the age-old Tamilian path of *bhakti* (devotion) consisting of smearing oneself with holy ashes, worship of Śiva, *japa* of His name, etc. in *Tevāram*.

It is significant to note that none of these ancient Śaiva saints, Tirumūlar, Appar or Saṁbandhar underestimate Mahā Viṣṇu.

Māṇikka-Vācakar (AD *660-92)*

The Dravidian spelling is *Maṇikka-Vāsagar* but I follow Surendranath Dasgupta's Sanskritised form *Vācakar*. It means 'a person of rubylike (precious) speech'. It may be his later title, but *PP* (*Periya Purāṇa*) accepts it as a personal name.

Māṇikka-Vācakar was an officer of Pāṇḍya King Arimardana of Madura. The king became a disciple of his servant-saint Māṇikka-Vācakar. He abdicated his kingdom in favour of his son and led a pious life. Māṇikka-Vācakar then went to Chidambaram which was then a centre of Buddhism. There he had a religious disputation with Buddhists. But accounts of the disputation show that neither side knew much of Buddhism. S.N. Dasgupta doubts whether such disputations could oust Buddhism from Tamil Nadu.[9]

The *Tiru-Vācaka* (*TV*) is a book of poems by Māṇikka Vācakar. It is full of devotional sentiments and philosophical ideas. There he describes his spiritual progress.[10] In *Śiva Purāṇam* section, he describes his realization of the beginningless and endless Śiva as dwelling in his heart and Śiva's dance, etc. were of the god in his heart. Śiva is embodiment of Bliss. After purification, i.e., removal of *malas*, he experiences God as Supreme Effulgence (*parañjyoti*). He finally reaches the stage called *ānandātīta* (beyond bliss) and realizes the *parāparam* (Supreme-most Śiva).

Māṇikka-Vācakar's teaching as gleaned from his songs (verses) are as follows :

> He accepts the fundamental triad of *pati, paśu, pāśa*. It is due to Śiva's grace (Tamil — *Aruḷ*) that an individual can progress spiritually and all the three *malas* (*pāśas* or bonds) viz *āṇava, kārma* and *māyīya* are completely removed. The individual soul becomes free and stays in spiritual bliss in the vicinity of Śiva. Spiritual preceptor (*guru*) is needed for the destruction or disappearance of the object of knowledge (*jñeya*), the knower (*jñātā*) and knowledge (*jñāna*) in the *samādhi* stage, and the need of Śiva's grace for *mokṣa*.[11]

As noted by S.N. Dasgupta, all the characteristics of *SŚ* are detailed in the *Vāyavīya Saṁhitā* of *Śiva Mahāpurāṇa*.

Sundar or Sundarmūrti[12] *(circa* AD *716-35)*

Sundar or Sundaramūrti, the boy-saint is regarded as the ideal of *sakhā mārga* (*sakhya bhakti*). Not merely from the mythological *PP*, but information gleaned from his songs, we find him requesting Śiva pleasures in life including a girl (called) Śāṅgilī and Śiva granted it. He lost his eyesight after marriage with Śaṅgilī and he requested Śiva 'to give a stick' (v. 54.4). He blames Śiva for his blindness : "O God, you made me blind for Śāṅgilī" (v. 63.4). He complains : "O Lord, I try to speak with women but they discard me calling me a blind man. It is so humiliating, O Lord." (v. 9) But his other verses are noted for intense devotional fervour couched in the sweetest language.

Sundar went as a guest to King Cermān Perumal. There he prayed Śiva for taking him to Kailāsa. The request was promptly granted by Śiva. He was only eighteen years old then.

These Tamilian saints were ardent devotees. They were not experts in Vedic lore but were familiar with Purāṇic legends about Śiva. They gave philosophical turns to these legends to suit the Śaivite cases. (For example, Śiva-Mohinī incident at the basis of the concept of *Hari-Hara* icon with a view to emphasize the identity of Śiva and Viṣṇu.

There is, however, no systematic treatment of the system of Siddhānta Śaivism in Tamil then. It was in the thirteenth century AD and after that great *Sanātanācārya*s like Aghora Śiva, Meyakandadeva, Aruṇa Nandi, Umāpati Śivācārya who produced systematic treatises on Śiddhānta Śaivism (in Tamil and Sanskrit).

But some three to four centuries before the Tamil *Sanātanācāryas*, we have a standard systematic treatise on Siddhānta Śaivism called *Tattva Prakāśa* by King Bhoja of Dhara (AD 1018-63). It is commented upon by Kumāradeva and Aghora Śiva — the great *Sanātanācārya* of *SŚ* of Tamil Nadu. This work is cited as authority in the *Śaiva-darśana* section of *Sarvadarśana-Saṅgraha* of Mādhavācārya.

Siddhānta Śaivism in Tattva-Prakāśa

Like other schools of Śaivism, this school subscribes to the theory of three categories viz. *pati, paśu* and *pāśa*. (In Tamil, *Irāi, Uyir* and *Kaṭṭu*). Mādhava, in *Sarva-darśana-Saṅgraha* (*Sds*) calls *SŚ* 'a *Mahā-Tantra*' with three categories and four feet.[13] Bhojadeva differs from others and adds to the usual three *pāśa*s viz. (1) (*āṇava*) *mala*, (2) *karma* and (3) *māyā*, two more *pāśas* viz. (4) the world created by *māyā* and (5) *tirodhāna* (power to conceal) and designates this group as *Arthapañcaka* in *Tattva-Prakāśa* (*TP*). In fact (3) and (4) are the subtle and gross aspects of *māyā* and (5) is inclusion of Śiva's power of *tirodhāna* as a *pāśa* — a point emphasized by Kumāradeva in *Tātparya-dīpikā* (*TD*) a commentary on *TP*.

Though consciousness or *caitanya* is a common factor between *pati* (Śiva) and *paśu* (souls), the latter are bound by *saṁsāra* and include everyone from god Brahmā to immobiles in this category, Śiva being their controller is hence called *Paśupati*.[15]

In the very introduction of *TP*, Bhojadeva states : Śiva is essentially *cit* (consciousness), omnipresent, eternal one, bliss incarnate (Śaṁbhu), bestower of grace on all, quiescent, self-luminous (ever-illuminating) — master (i.e., of unobstructed sovereignty), the sole seed of the universe.[16] He is called Śiva as he is untouched by the beginningless (*āṇava*) *mala*.[17] He is disinterested (*udāsīna*) but by his very presence the universe is created, as rice-grains are turned into food by the presence of fire though not touched by it.[18] *SŚ* differs considerably from *KŚ*, in explaining world-creation. In *KŚ*, Śiva is endowed with *prakāśa* and *vimarśa*. By his sheer will-power, without any *upādāna* (material cause or any other agency). Śiva creates (etc.) the universe. In *SŚ* Śiva is the operative or efficient cause (like a potter) and *māyā* is the material cause (clay in case of a pot) and Śiva's *śakti*s serve as *kāraṇa* or instrumental cause. It is the *Prakṛti-pariṇāma-vāda* and not *Brahma-pariṇāma-vāda* as in the *Vedānta*.

In *SŚ*, *māyā* is real and not *mithyā* as in *Sāṅkara Vedānta*. *Māyā* is a subtle *prakṛti* and hence an invisible material cause[19] which pervades everything (i.e., its products) from *kāla* (time) down to the gross element, earth. Just as earth (clay) pervades the entire (earthen) pot[20] Bhojadeva firmly refutes the attempts of the author of *Ratnatraya* to regard *māyā* as a part of Śiva. He states, when you accept *māyā* as the material cause (*upādāna*) and try to identify it with operative cause (Śiva), you cannot explain the creation of the universe.[21] To argue that Śiva and His powers (for example *māyā*) are related to each other by *dharma-dharmī* relation, it gives the credit if creation to powers (*māyā*) and Śiva, the basis (*dharmin*) of powers is reduced to non-entity — an absurd position.[22] Bhojadeva concludes that *māyā*, though *mūlaprakṛti* (initial primordial nature) is after all an *upādāna* — and is different from Śiva.

A few more peculiar concepts about Śiva may be mentioned :

(1) *Nirguṇatva* does not mean 'attributelessness' of Śiva. It means that Śiva is devoid of the *guṇas* of *māyā* viz. *sattva, rajas* and *tamas*.[23]

(2) *Nirākāratva* does not mean 'formlessness' but that Śiva pervades all forms. *Pauṣkarāgama* says: "How can one's intelligence grasp a formless object".[24] To solve this problem of devotees who wish to adore Śiva, Śiva was presumed to have a body consisting of the five *mantras* from the *Taittirīya Āraṇyaka*, 17.1-5 which form the basis of the *Pāśupata* school. The five *mantras*, the *pratīkas* (opening word) of which are: *iśāna* forms the countenance or face of Śiva, *tatpuruṣāya*, the heart, *aghora*, the secret part, and the like. But this is an imaginative theorizing. The *Liṅga Purāṇa* identifies Śiva's person with *oṁkāra* with the *Ṛgveda* as the mouth, *Sāmaveda* as the tongue and the like. The *Pauṣkarāgama* is conscious of this imaginative theorization and concludes: "such a form is remembered to be such for the protection of the aspirant"[26] (*sādhaka*). Further it addresses Śiva : "You with a form can be appreciated. The intellect cannot grasp a formless entity".[27]

It is with such a body constituted of *mantras* that Śiva performs the five functions: viz. creation (sending out of himself the universe), sustenance, withdrawal (of the universe within Him), concealment and grace (to grant *mokṣa*).

Māṇikka-Vācakar who supports the ancient concept of *aṣṭamūrti* Śiva (Śiva pervading eight forms viz. the five elements, the sun, the moon and the sentient man) firmly states that Śiva transcends these forms and has no name, no forms and no characteristic marks.

(3) *The svātantrya-vāda* : According to *KŚ*, *svātantrya* means absolute free-will or *vimarśa*. But in *SŚ*, it means 'not being subject to the instruction of others'. Śiva is thus free but he dispenses fruits or results according to the *karmas* of the *jīivas*.[28] Due to such dispensation, Śiva cannot be charged with partiality (*vaiṣamya*) or cruelty (*nairghṛṇya*). Just as the sun spreads his rays equally all over the world, some lotuses bloom immediately and some late according to their nature but the sun treats all equally.[29] This is not *niyativāda* as Śiva exercises his power and grace and grants *mokṣa* to the deserving. He exercises his functions to help *paśus* to attain *mokṣa*. The term Śiva was later extended to spiritually advanced souls, called *Mantra Mantreśvara*, and released souls also.

Paśu (Individual Soul)

We have seen (*supra* pp. 12-13) that individual souls are not born or created and that originally they are of the same status as that of Śiva. It is due to *malas* or *pāśas* (bonds) that their powers are severely restricted and from the point of powers as *jīvātman* (individual soul) is like an atom. "When freed from the bonds through the grace of Śiva, they become veritable Śiva."[30] As noted before (*supra* p. 14) the unanswered question is how Śiva(s) got bound or sullied with the so-called beginningless *āṇava mala* and why *Parama* Śiva bound the *jīvātmans* at all. As the concept of *pāśa* (bondage) or *mala* is already discussed (*supra* pp. 13-15) we proceed with the classification of these *paśus*. *Paśus* are classified according to their bondages (*malas*) as follows:[31]

1. *Vijñānakala* : Sullied with the beginningless *āṇava mala*.
2. *Pralayākala* : Bound with *āṇava* and *karma malas*.
3. *Sakala* : Bound with *āṇava, karma* and *māyā malas*.

Here *kalā* means 'a part or a particle referring to the condition of empirical existence'.

Sakala-jīva is the soul with all the empirical conditions of existence and is associated with all the three bonds (*malas*). The concept of *pralayākala jīva* is peculier. It means the condition of a *jīva* during the period of a *pralaya* when the universe is dissolved. As there is no existence of *māyā* during that period, the *jīva* has only two bonds viz. *āṇava* and *kārma* (*karmas* do not get destroyed during the *pralaya*). After the period of the *pralaya*, *pralayākala* becomes *sakala*. The *vijñānakala jīvas* (with *āṇava mala* only) remain in the region of *śuddha māyā* till they get *Śiva-mukti* through Śiva's grace. They are not born again in *saṁsāra*.

Another belief is that Śiva gives some spiritual knowledge to these spiritually advanced people and appoints them on the posts of *vidyeśvara* (masters of *vidyā*).

After *pralaya*, those *jīvas* whose *āṇava* and *karma malas* are not mature, get a *pūryaṣṭaka* body (body constituted of eight elements) according to their *karma* and are born in different species,[33] to experience the fruits of their actions.

In his commentary on *TP,* 1-11 and 12, the commentator Kumāradeva enumerates the constituents of *pūryaṣṭaka* or *liṅga-śarīra* as follows:

(1) Five sense-organs of sound, touch, form, taste and smell, (i.e., the physical apparatus) *plus* the psychic apparatus viz. *manas* (mind), *buddhi* (intelligene) and *ahaṁkāra* (ego, 'I'ness).

(2) He quotes another source which is more extensive. "The eight constituents" are as follows :

(1) Five conative sense-organs, (2) Five congnitive organs, (3) Group of four psychic apparatus like mind, intelligence, etc., (4) Five vital airs, (5) Five *tanmātras*, (6) *kāma* (desire), (7) *karma* (action) and (8) *avidyā*.[34]

Pūryaṣṭaka is a special term used by *SŚ* for the Purāṇic term *liṅga-śarīra*, *KŚ* however, is silent about its constituents.

Pāśa (Bondage)

All sects of Śaivism accept three *malas* or *pāśas* viz. *āṇava*, *karma,* and *māyā*. But *SŚ* adds *tirodhāna* (concealment) as the fourth *pāśa*. The last is the power of Śiva, and not that of a *jīvātman*. As the topic is discussed in details (*supra* pp. 13-15, 47-49) it will be briefly noted here about *māyā* some special points may be noted.

Like other Śaiva sects *SŚ* uses the terms *mala*, *ajñāna*, etc. for the first (i.e., *āṇava*) *mala*. As *TP,* 1.17 states, it conceals the powers of knowledge and action (*jñānaśakti* and *kriyāśakti*). It is beginningless like husk on the grain or green patina on copper but can be wiped out by spiritual knowledge (*jñāna-nivartya*).[35] Though *āṇava mala* is not completely washed off, some souls are spiritually advanced. Śiva, out of grace, appoints them on some *vidyeśvara* post. Hence it is called *adhikāra mala*.

Karma

Karma is regarded as a powerful bondage from which it is difficult to extricate oneself. It drags the souls like beasts.[36] It is beginningless like seed-sprout continuity. It is of two types: (i) *dharma* conferring merits and (ii) *adharma* resulting in sins—*dharma-karmas* are *iṣṭa,* i.e., Vedic and *pūrta—karmas* are tāntric. Dhārmic acts are *nitya* (to be observed daily like *agnihotra* — fire-worship), *naimittika* (occasional, e.g. performance of *iṣṭi* after the birth of a son) and *kāmya* performed with some desire (such as performing sacrifices for getting a place into heaven). By non-performance of dhārmic acts and committing immoral deeds, the person contracts sin. (*TP,* p. 59) Both merits and sins are bondages which condition the transmigration of the soul. It is Śiva's grace which releases man from this bond.

By the way, it may be noted that Kumāradeva has not consulted *Smṛti* texts and defined *iṣṭa* and *pūrta dharmas*. According to *Smṛtis*, *pūrta-dharmas* are works of public utility such as digging wells, construction of temples, while *iṣṭa-dharmas* include *agnihotra*, recitation of *Vedas*, performance of penance (*vide Atri Smṛti* 43, 44).

Concept of Māyā

According to *SŚ māyā* is the material cause of the universe. It is real and eternal.[37] The *Śaiva Siddhāntas* believe in *sat-kārya-vāda* (the necessary existence of an effect inherent in the cause.) The world is non-intelligent (*a-cit*), so its material cause *māyā* is *a-cit*. Hence, by itself, it cannot create unless it is activated by some intelligent one (*cid-vastu*) which is Śiva. Conversely Śiva by himself cannot create the world — unless both Śiva and *māyā* are united.[38]

Śiva alone is *sat-*, *māyā* is different from, other than, Śiva, hence *a-sat*. The term *a-sat* does **not** mean 'non-existent'. Not only is *māyā* real (*vastu-rūpā*) but its products or effects, the *tattvas* and the world are real (*TP*, pp. 71-72).

They derive the term *māyā* from two roots — √*mā* and √*yā*. *Mā* = 'one in which everything is dissolved'. *Yā* = 'that from which everything goes out' (is produced or created). It provides the soul with a body (*tanu*), sense-organs, objects of enjoyment. Activated by the power of intelligence (*cicchakti*) of Śiva, it creates the universe. It is due to its power of delusion that *māyā* is regarded as a bond.[39]

SŚ regards two grades of *māyā* : (1) Pure and (2) Impure.

PURE — ŚUDDHA, OR MAHĀMĀYĀ

It is untouched by *āṇava* and *karma malas*. By his powers: *icchā* (wish or desire), *jñāna* (knowledge), *kriyā* (will or action), Śiva creates from *śuddha-māyā*, *nāda*, *bindu*, *sādākhya*, *māheśvarī* and *śuddha vidyā*. *Nāda* is *śiva-tattva*, *bindu* is *śakti-tattva*. *Nāda* is due to the operation of *jñāna-śakti* on *śuddha-māyā* and *bindu* arises when *kriyā-śakti* operates on *nāda*. When *jñāna* and *kriyā-śakti* operate on *bindu* in equal measure *sādākhya* is created. *māheśvarī* is derived from this, when more of *kriyā-śakti* operates along with *jñāna*. *Śuddha-vidyā* is evolved from *māheśvarī* when *jñāna-śakti* is a dominant factor.

The group of the above five evolutes of *śuddha vidyā* are called *Śiva-tattvas* or *preraka kāṇḍa*. The terms *śiva, śakti, śadāśiva, vidyā* have different implications in *KŚ* as Śiva is both *nimitta* and *upādāna kāraṇas* in *KŚ*. *SŚ* holds that it is from *śuddha māyā* that the system of sounds, *parā, paśyantī, madhyamā* and *vaikharī* are evolved. *Parā* is the subtle, supreme sound and is located in the navel region of man. *Paśyantī* is a grosser, undifferentiated sound somewhere in the region of the heart. *Madhyamā* is grosser still but not articulate. It is presumed to be in the throat region. *Vaikharī* is the articulate sound we produce with our mouths. Meaning (import) is communicated by a *śakti* manifested with letters and words. This capacity is called *sphoṭa* by grammarians. The remaining *tattvas* (given in Appendix III of chapter 1) are the evolutes of *aśuddha māyā* or *mohinī* (the deluder). Due to the impurity of this *māyā*, Śiva does not operate on it. Sadāśiva produces from *aśuddha-māyā* three *tattvas* viz. *kāla* (time), *niyati* (destiny), *kalā* (a digit or a particle) and from *kalā*, two more *tattvas* (principles) viz. *vidyā* (knowledge) and *rāga* (attachment) evolve. These five *tattvas* constitute the sheaths or *kañcukas* of the soul. The soul as conditioned by these *tattvas* becomes *puruṣa tattva*.

The counterpart of *puruṣa* is *prakṛti*. It arises out of *kalā* by the operation of Rudra. The five sheaths along with *puruṣa* and *prakṛti* are known as *vidyā tattvas*. They are called *bhojayitṛ kāṇḍa* — the part of evolution causing enjoyment. *Citta* (mind) and *buddhi* (intellect) are the evolutes of *prakṛti* in its unmanifest (*avyakta*) stage. From *buddhi* is evolved *ahaṁkāra* (ego, I-ness). There are three varieties of *ahaṁkāra* — that which is predominated by *sattva-guṇa* is *taijasa*, by *rajo-guṇa* is *vaikṛta* and by *tamo-guṇa, bhūtādi*. It should be noted that *Sāṅkhyas* call *sāttvika ahaṁkāra* as *vaikṛta* and the *rājasa ahaṁikāra* as *taijasa*.

From *taijasa ahaṁkāra* are evolved organs of senses and *manas* (mind), from *vaikṛta ahaṁkāra* conative organs and from *bhūtādi*, the subtle elements called *tan-mātras*.*

The above discussion shows the close relation between *māyā* and the *tattvas*. We have seen that *māyā* as a *mala* or bondage of the soul provides the soul with the body, locations and objects of enjoyment. It is called *bhogya-kāṇḍa*.

---

*Refer to *tattvas* (*supra* pp. 16-17 and Appendix III (*supra* p. 26). The whole matter is esoteric theorizing.

Nirodha or Tirodhāna

To the usual list of three *pāśas*, Bhojadeva adds the fourth *pāśa* viz. *tirodhāna*. To justify this addition, he says that *pāśas* (bonds) are themselves insentient. It is Śiva who infuses the power (*āveśa*) of restricting the original Śiva-like powers of the *jīvātman* (soul). This restricting power (*puruṣa-tirodhāyikā*) is in a sense a bondage. Hence four *pāśas* should be recognised.[40]

Bhojadeva at one place (*TP*, p. 33) accepts five *pāśas* viz. *mala* (*āṇava*), *karma*, *māyā*, the world created by *māyā* and *tirodhāna*. His commentator Kumāradeva tries to defend him by saying that the gross (*sthūla*) *māyā* and subtle (*sūkṣma*) *māyā* constitute but one *pāśa*. Hence the number of *paśas* remain[41] four only.

The Paths to Mokṣa (Liberation)

Śaivism is no arm-chair philosophy. It is meant for liberation from *saṁsāra* and as such has prescribed paths to *mokṣa*. They have used the terms *caryā*, *kriya*, *yoga* and *jñāna* which are used for the parts of *Āgama* texts. They hold that these terms stand for the four consecutive paths to Liberation. They are :

DĀSA MĀRGA (CORRESPONDING TO DĀSYA BHAKTI OF NINEFOLD PATH OF BHAKTI)

The aspirant is to cleanse the Śiva Temple, worship Śiva — icon or Liṅga — present therein, sing eulogies or *stotras* of Śiva, to render physical service to devotees of Śiva who in a way represent god Śiva himself. This is the *caryā* path.

SAT-PUTRA MĀRGA

In due course, the services as a servant of Śiva create affection for the lord as a son feels for his father. This **qualitative change** in rendering service to Śiva is important. This corresponds to *kriyā*.

SAKHĀ-MĀRGA (CORRESPONDING TO SAKHYA BHAKTI OF THE NINEFOLD DIVISION)

In this stage, by practice of yogic practices such as *pratyāhāra, dhyāna, dhāraṇā*, the aspirant establishes internal intimate relation with God. The main difference from the previous two paths and this is that they are external. Here, in this path of contemplation, senses are withdrawn from external objects and the mind is concentrated on Śiva.

These three paths are preparatory to the final *san-mārga*, the path of knowledge of *sat,* i.e., Śiva. It is at this stage that by Śiva's grace, the beginningless (*āṇava*) *mala* is washed out and the soul (*jīvātman*) attains *śivatva* — **not** complete Śivahood. The soul is not completely absorbed in Śiva as believed by *Advaitins* of Śaṅkara School. *SŚ* believes that the *pati-jñāna* in the *mokṣa* stage is the soul's knowledge through the Lord.

It is believed that the successful completion of these stages (which are mutually inter-linked) lead to the types of liberation called *salokatā* (stay in the same region as that of Śiva) *samīpatā* (stay in proximity to the Lord), *sarūpatā* (similarity in appearance like the Lord) and *sāyujyatā* (not absorption in Śiva but *Śivatva* — the bliss of Śivahood. Such *jīvātman* has not the capacity to wield Śiva's five functions — from creation to conferment of grace on the devotee).

Presentation in Tamil Literature[42]

In *Śaiva Siddhānta* Literature in Tamil the spiritual progress of the aspirant is given as follows :

The soul must equate the two types of *karmas* — good (*puṇya*) and evil (*pāpa*) — as both constitute the bond — *karma*. When such an attitude — indifference to merit and demerit — is confirmed, it is the *mala-paripāka* (maturation of the *mala*). At this stage the soul no longer cognizes with the evolutes of *aśuddha māyā* nor with its own feeble intelligence. The soul has no use now for *pāśa jñāna* and *paśu-jñāna* as it is now filled with glory of Śiva through contemplation. Now God blesses him with his grace called *śakti-nipāta* (the descent of Śiva's power). After this descent of Śiva's grace, Śiva reveals Himself to the aspirant soul and imparts to him the knowledge (*jñāna*) that liberates him. The soul is now in the *jñāna-mārga* in *śuddha avasthā* in the state of grace (Tamil *Aruḷ*). This state is different from *kevala avasthā* (a state of darkness (or Tam. *Iruḷ*) and the *sakala avasthā* — a state of confused knowledge (Tam. *Maruḷ*). The soul in the *Śuddha avasthā* is *vijñānakala* to whom Śiva manifests Himself as its (soul's) inner light. To *pralayākala* souls, Śiva appears in a divine supernatural form and to the *sakala jīva*, he appears as a human *guru* (spiritual preceptor). He gives the *sakala jīva*, *dīkṣā*, weans him away from association with *mala*s and makes him realize him own *Śivatva*.

SŚ believes in *jīvan-mukti* — liberation within the lifetime of *jīva*. During the remaining part of life, such a person experiences the residue of his *prārabdha karma* but it does not affect the soul's perfection.

Concept of Mokṣa

SŚ does not believe in the complete absorption of the *jīva* (soul) in Śiva as believed in *Advaita*. *SŚ* believes that in the *mokṣa* stage, the individual soul retains his identity but enjoys the bliss of Śivahood. He does not have the power to exercise the five exclusive functions (from creation to grace) of God. As all his *mala*s are removed, he does not revert to *saṁsāra*. This stage is the superior (*para*) *mokṣa* stage. In case of those whose *karma* and *māyā mala*s are destroyed but there is some slight residue of *āṇava mala* have a body created from *bindu*. Śiva appoints such advanced souls on *vidyeśvarī* posts. These souls are in the *apara* (lower stage) of *mokṣa*. With *SŚ* *mokṣa* (liberation) is not a negative concept of *duḥkhānta* but a positive Śiva-like blissful state.

As noted in the Introduction (*supra* p. 1) it is interesting to compare the speculations of this Dualistic Śaivism with Dualistic Vaiṣṇavism of Madhva.

(1) Like *SŚ*, Madhva affirms the multiplicity of souls, the difference between God and Souls, difference between souls *inter se* and between matter, souls and God. God is independent while souls and matter are dependent on God.

(2) Like *SŚ*, Madhva believes that in the creation of the universe, God is the efficient cause (*nimitta kāraṇa*) like a potter, clay or earth is the material cause (*upādāna*) and other *śakti*s (like the stick that moves the potter's wheel) are the instrumental cause.

(3) Importance of *bhakti* for obtaining supreme spiritual knowledge and the necessity of the descent of God's grace (*anugraha*) for liberation.

Notes

1. *siddhānta-śabdaḥ . . . yoga-rūḍhyā śiva-praṇīteṣu kāmikādiṣu daśāṣṭā-daśasu tantreṣu prasiddhaḥ* ।
   Bhoga-Kārikā, 2 (Quoted by K. C. Pande in *Bhāskarī*)
2. *ruru-siddhānta-saṁsiddhau bhoga-mokṣau sa-sādhanau*
   vacmī sādhaka-bodhāya leśato yukti-sanskṛtau
   — *Mokṣa-Kārikā*, 79
3. C.V. Narayan Aiyyar, *Origin and Early History of Śaivism in South India*, pp. 224 ff.
4. *Op. cit.* (summarised from the section on *Tirumandirum*) pp. 247-84.
5. *Op. cit.* pp. 423-31, 444-662 for these dates.
6. *Op. cit.* pp. 372-74.
7. *yato vā imāni bhūtāni jāyante* ।
   yena tātāni jīvanti ।
   yat prayānty abhisaṁviśanti ।

tad vijijñāsasva tad brahmeti ।

— *Taittirīya Upaniṣad*, 3.1

8. *adṛśyam . . agrāhyam alakṣaṇam*
acintyam . . . śāntam śivam
advaitam . . . sa ātmā sa vijñeyaḥ ।

— *Māṇḍūkya Upaniṣad*, 7

9. S.N. Dasgupta, *History of Indian Philosophy* , V p. 154.
10. C.V.N. Aiyyar, *op. cit* pp. 436-39.
11. S.N. Dasgupta, *op. cit.* pp. 149-59.
12. C.V.N. Aiyyar, *op. cit.* pp. 444-62.
13. Mādhava, *Sarva-darśana-saṅgraha* (*Sds*) p. 77.
14. *TP*, p. 32.
15. *Liṅga Purāṇa* (quoted in *TD*, p. 31).
16. *cidghana eko vyāpī nityaḥ satatoditaḥ prabhuḥ śāntaḥ* ।
jayati jagadeka bījam sarvānugrahakaḥ śambhuḥ ॥

— *TD*, 1-1

17. *anādi-mala-saṁśleṣa-prāga-bhāvāt svabhāvataḥ* ।
atyanta-pariśuddhātmā-ityato' yam śiva ucyate ॥

— *Vāyavīya Saṁhitā* (quoted in *TP*, p. 42)

18. *yathā hyavikriyo vahnir jalataṇḍula-vikriyām* ।
tathā karotyudāsīnaḥ śambhur māyādi-vikriyām.

— *TP*, p. 46

19. *māyopadānam mṛt-tantvādi-sthānīyam . . . sūkṣmatvād anupalaṁbho māyāyā na asattvāt* ।

— *TP*, p. 111

20. *vyāpini-ghaṭa-śarāva-kumbhādiṣu mṛdvat, svakāryeṣu kālādyavani-anteṣu jaḍatayā'nusyūtā*

— *TP*, p. 114

21. *tasyā upādānāntarābhāvena akāryatvāt* ।
tadabhāve cānavasthā prasaṅgaḥ ।"*eteṣāmeva pāśānaṁ māyā kāraṇamucyate* । *mūla-prakṛtir avyaktā" iti māyayā mūla-prakṛtitvopādānācca siddham* ।

— *TP*, p. 113

TP, re-affirms this view on p. 117.

22. *śakter dharmatvenāśrayaṁ vinā avasthānāsaṁbhavāt tadāśrayaḥ sa eva śaktimān saṅkalpa-mātreṇa viśvakartā* ।

— *Ratnatraya*, 103

23. T.M. Mahādevan, *History of Philosophy Eastern & Western* vol. I., p. 371 (*Meykaṇḍa* quoted here).

24. Quoted by Mādhav *Sds*, p. 80.
25. *pañca-mantra-tamus śrīmān sakalam paripaṭhyate* ।
īśāna-mūrdhā, 'puṁ'-vaktro ।
hy'aghora' hṛdayaḥ prabhuḥ ।
ucyate 'vāma'-guhyo'yam 'sadyo-mūrtr maheśvaraḥ ।
evaṁ mantrāstū pañcaite yair nibaddha-toṇuh śivā
— *TP*, p. 43
26. *sādhakasya tu rakṣārtham*
tasya rūpam idam smrtam ।
— *Pauṣkarāgama* (Quoted in *Sds*, p. 80)
27. *ākāra-vāns tvam niyamād upāsyo*
na vastvanākāram upaiti buddhiḥ
— Quoted in *Sds*. p. 80
28. *svatantrasyāprayojyatvam karaṇādi-prayoktṛtā*
kartaḥ svātantryam etad hi na karmādyanapekṣatā
— *Sds*, p. 78
29. *anugraha-svabhāvatve na sarvān mocayet śivaḥ* ।
svabhāvo'pi hī bhāvānām bhāvino'rthasya kāraṇam ।
svayaṁ na vikasantyeva sva-svabhāvānurodhataḥ ।
evam pakva-malāneva mocayen na śivaḥ parān ।।
— *Vāyavīya Saṁhitā* quoted in *TP*
30. *muktātmāno'pi śivāḥ*
kintvete tat-prasādato muktāḥ ।
— *TP* (Quoted in *Sds*, p. 81)
31. After enumerating and naming the classes, Soma-Śaṁbhu states —
tatrādyo mala-mātreṇa yukto'nyo mala karmabhiḥ ।
kalādi-bhūmi-paryanta-tatvais tu sakalo yutaḥ ।
— Quoted in *Sds*., p. 82
32. *ādyān anugṛhya vidyeśatvam niyojayatyaṣṭau* ।
— *TP*, p. 1-10, p. 49
The list of eight 'offices' of Vidyeśvaras is quoted from '*Bahudaivata*' in *Sds*, p. 81.
33. *pralayākaleṣu yeṣāṁ pakve mala-karmaṇī vrajantyanye* ।
pūryāṣṭaka-deha-yutā yoniṣu nikhilāsu karma vas'āt ।।
— *TP*, 1-11
Also
buddhān śesānakhilān viniyuṅkte bhoga-bhuktaye puṁsaḥ ।
tat-karmaṇānugamāt ।
— *TP*, p. 1-16; *TD* on *TP* 1.13, p. 51

34. *TD* on *TP*, 1.13, p. 52.
35. *eko hyaneka-śaktir dṛk-kriyayoś chādako malo puṁsām* ।
tuṣa-kaṁbukavaj jñeyaḥ tāmrāśrita-kālimāvad vā ।।
— *TP*, 1-17
36. *karmākhyo'yaṁ mahā-pāśo durmocas ten jantavaḥ* ।
itastataḥ samākṛṣya nīyante paśava iva ।
— *Siddhānta-hṛdaya* (Quoted by Kumāra on *TP*, 1-18, p. 60)
37. *māyā to vasturūpā mūlaṁ viśvasya, nityā sā* ।
— *TP*, 1-18
38. *māyā tāvan na parameśvarānadhiṣṭhitā jaḍā jagad upādānam bhavati* । *maheśvaraś cetano'pi māyām vinā* । *na viśvamūlatāṁ bhajate nir-vyāpārodāsīna-mātratvād iti tayoḥ saṁsṛṣṭayoreva jagan-mūlatvam* ।
— *TP*, p. 62
39. *moha-hetutvād viparīta-pratipattihetunā māyākhyena bandhanena bhāvyam* — *Ratnatraya* (quoted in *Bhāskarī*)
40. *pāśānugrāhitvāt puruṣa-tirodhāyikā vibhoḥ śaktiḥ* ।
pāśatvenābhihitā pāśaś ca catur vidhās tvevam ।।
— *TP*, 1-19
41. *sthūla-sūkṣma-vibhāgenoktāyā māyāyā ekatva-vivakṣayā cāturvidhyābhidhānād iti* । — *TD* on *TP*, 1-19, p. 73
42. Summarised from T.M.P. Mahādevan's article in *The History of Philosophy Eastern and Western*, p. 378.

5

Śivādvaita
(Śaiva Viśiṣṭādvaita of Śrīkaṇṭha)

We have seen that while solving the riddle of life, the main problem of Indian thinkers (whether Śaiva or Vaiṣṇava) has been how to determine the relation between unity and plurality, God and the world which consists of sentients (*cit*) and non-sentients (*a-cit*). Monists of Śaṅkara school declared that the *Brahman* alone is Real and the Plurality (of the world) is *mithyā* — an enigmatic (and hence untranslatable) term. S.N. Dasgupta has devoted more than 100 pages as to how this term generated a controversy between Vaiṣṇava Dualists and Monists for some generations. (*History of Indian Philosophy,* Vol. IV, pp. 204-315).

In Śaivism, Vasugupta's *Īśvarādvaya Vāda* advocated the concept of Śiva which was wider than Śaṅkara's concept of the *Brahman*. *Māyā* of Śaṅkarite philosophy was superfluous in *KŚ* as Śiva possessed both *prakāśa* and *vimarśa* powers. But Pluralistic Realism of *Siddhānta Śaivas*, despite some loose ends in their metaphysics, appealed to the masses in Tamil Nadu.

The one common factor between the above two schools is their Āgamic authority. The Śaiva authors however, equate the *Āgama* and the *Veda* as authoritative texts, as

Lord Śiva is the author of them both. Even some *Āgama* texts claim to contain the essence of the *Vedas*. For example, the *Makuṭāgama* says "This *Tantra* is the essence of the *Veda*" :

veda-sāraṁ idaṁ tantram ।

Another *Āgama* — *Suprabhedāgama* states that the teaching of *Āgama* (*Siddhānta*) is the essence of the *Veda*:

siddhānto vedasāratvāt ।

Modern scholars however differ.

One more attempt of reconciling unity and plurality is attributed to a post-Śaṅkara commentator of *BrS* — Bhāskara who holds that there may be plurality or difference in the effects but there is non-difference (*a-bheda*) in the cause (*kāraṇa*).[1] It is however a pre-*Brahma Sūtra* teacher, Āśmarathya who advocated this *bhedā-bheda* (difference-cum-non-difference) theory. Referring to *BrS,* 1.2.29 and 1.4.20. S. Radhakrishnan explains : "The soul is neither different nor non-different from the *Brahman* even as the sparks (flying away from fire) are neither different nor non-different from the fire. The relation (between the two) is not of absolute identity but of cause and effect" — a view endorsed by commentators of *BrS* like Bhartṛprapañca. Bhāskara, Rāmānuja and Nimbārka.[2]

The next stage is to regard that the sentients (*cit*) and non-sentients (*a-cit*) though different are, parts of God's body (Śiva or Viṣṇu) and are related mutually.

Śrīkaṇṭha, the exponent of *Śivādvaita*, adopts this view. In the conclusion of his commentary on *Pariṇāmāt* (*BrS,* 1.4.27) he states :

> It is logical to hold that the Supreme God is characterised by the sentients (*cit*) and non-sentients (*a-cit*). He is both the cause and

> the effect according to the special state or condition.[3]

Rāmānuja also holds that Viṣṇu Nārāyaṇa designated as *Brahman* which is characterised both by sentience and non-sentience, is the only Reality (*tattvam*). I shall point out later that Śrīkaṇṭha, though an exponent of *Viśiṣṭādvaita* is not a follower of Rāmānuja.

Śrīkaṇṭha : His magnum opus Brahma-mīmāṁsā Bhāṣya

Very little is known about the life of Śrīkaṇṭha. He does not mention the name of any commentator of *BrS* like Śaṅkara. Rāmānuja, etc. In the introduction to his commentary on the *BrS* the *Brahma-mīmāṁsā-bhāṣya* (*BMB*), he pays respects to his *guru* Śveta — an incarnation of Śiva in the first *Kaliyuga* of this *Manvantara*. Śveta has the following disciples viz. Śvetaśikha, Śvetāsya, Śvetalohita (*Kūrma Purāṇa,* I.51.4.13) — sheer mythology of little historical value.

As distinguished from teachers of *KŚ* and *ŚS* schools, he adopted *BrS* and not *Āgamas*, as the authoritative text to establish his *Śaiva Viśiṣṭādvaita* theory.

So we have to turn to internal evidence. In the introductory verse No. 5 of the *BMB*, he declares that his object of writing this commentary on *BrS* is 'to purify' the *BrS* 'polluted' by other previous authors (*ācāryas*).[4]

We can guess that the target of this criticism is Śaṅkara, Sūryanārāyaṇa Śāstrī's *Śivādvaita of Śrīkaṇṭha* (Appendix III.B) shows that there are 22 instances of resemblance between the *Bhāṣyas* of Śaṅkara and Śrīkaṇṭha while the number of differences between them is 84 — and many of them on important points. For example *BrS,* 1.1.2:

janmādyasya yataḥ ।

According to Śaṅkara, this *Sūtra* does not present an inferential argument but demonstrates (the reconciliation and harmonization) of different texts of the *Śruti*. As he poetically put it, the *śūtra* intends 'to string together the flowers in the form of the statements in the *Vedānta*'.[5]

Śrikaṇṭha refutes Śaṅkara's doctrine of the "attributelessness" (*nirguṇatva*) of the *Brahman*. The *Brahman* is the basis of all auspiciousness and is hence called *śiva-tattva*. The *Brahman* characterised by **subtle** sentients (*cit*) and non-sentients (*a-cit*) is the cause, while the *Brahman* characterised by **gross** sentients and non-sentients is the effect. Hence the decision (*siddhānta*) of this *sūtra* (*BrS*, 1.1.2) that the *Brahman* caused by the above (subtle-gross nature) is the cause of the creation, etc.[6]

(1) Further in Śrīkaṇṭha's commentary on the following *sūtras* :

(i) *jño'ta eva* (*BrS,* 2.1.18) in the *ārambhaṇa* section (*BrS,* 2.1.15-20 in *BMB,* II, p. 1-29) and

(ii) *kartā śāstrārthavat-tvāt* ।

(*BrS,* 2.3.33, *BMB,* III, p. 152)

Śrīkaṇṭha criticises Śaṅkara's view on the *ātman* (soul) and tries to prove the atomic nature (*aṇutva*), possession of knowledge (*jñātṛtva*) and being a doer (*kartṛtva*) of the *ātman*.[7]

The above is enough to show that Śrīkaṇṭha criticises Śaṅkara and hence belongs to post-Śaṅkara period.

2. There are two views about the contemporaneity of Rāmānuja and Śrīkaṇṭha. Both being advocates of *Viśiṣṭādvaita*, it is natural that there should be similarity in arguments. Possibly both must have used *Bodhāyana vṛtti*, one using it for Vaiṣṇavite views and the other for Śaivite view. Appaya Dīkṣita, commentator of Śrīkaṇṭha's

BMB, regards Śrīkaṇṭha the senior. Their philosophic views are compared later.

Discussing the problem of Śrīkaṇṭha's date in details, S.S. Sūryanārāyaṇa Śāstrī locates him in the twelfth century AD (*op. cit.,* p. 66). S.N. Dasgupta, C. Hayavadanarao and Jadunath Sinha assign him to the thirteenth century AD.

Śrīkaṇṭha's learned yet lucid commentary on the *BrS* is known as *Brahma-mīmāṁsā-Bhāṣya* (*BMB*). It was commented on by Nijaguṇa Śivayogī, Haradatta Śivācārya. Brahmavidyādharīndra and Appaya Dīkṣita. The commentary of Appaya Dīkṣita *Śivārkamaṇidīpa* is extant and published, while the others are lost. All these commentators are south Indians. I believe, like all other commentators on *BrS* like Śaṅkara to Vallalha, Śrīkaṇṭha must be in all probability a Southerner.

Śrīkaṇṭha — An Independent Thinker

We have seen above that Śrīkaṇṭha differs from Śaṅkara in the interpretation of the *BrS* about the nature and attributes of the *Brahman* and those of the soul (*ātman*). He knew *bhedābheda-vāda* (difference-cum-non-difference) advocated by Bhāskara (9th cent. AD). In this commentary on *adhikam tu bheda-nirdeśāt* (*BrS,* 2.1.22) he explains :

> Although there is non-difference in cause and effect and though the world consisting of sentients (*cit*) and non-sentients (*a-cit*) is the effect, the *bhedābheda-vāda* is not proved. We do not unhold absolute difference and non-difference between the *Brahman* and the phenomenal world. Nor do we hold *bhedābheda-vāda*.

Our position is that of *Viśiṣṭādvaitins* who regard their relation as that between the body and soul or *guṇa* and *quṇin* (attribute and the possessor of that attribute).[8]

Elsewhere Śrīkaṇṭha thinks that the person of God consists of both sentients (*cit*) and non-sentients (*a-cit*).[9]

Śrīkaṇṭha and Rāmānuja[10]

Both Śrīkaṇṭha and Rāmānuja advocated *Viśiṣṭādvaita*. It is hence natural that both of them should share some views in common. S.S. Sūryanārāyaṇa Śāstrī in his work on *Śivādvaita* has recorded systematically in the *sūtra*-wise order the points of resemblance between Śrīkaṇṭha's *BMB* and Rāmānuja's *Śrībhāṣya*. It is found that Śrīkaṇṭha agrees with Rāmānuja's interpretation of *sūtras* at 50 places (Appendix III.A to *op. cit* Sūryanārāyaṇa Śāstrī's *Śivādvaita*) but Śrīkaṇṭha treats 85 topics differently from Rāmānuja's *Śrībhāṣya* (Appendix IIIC to *op. cit.*).

It is not arithmetical majority of differences in interpretation. The topics so independently explained are important. For example

SUPERIORITY OF ŚIVA OVER NĀRĀYAṆA

Nārāyaṇa is not *Brahman*. He is the *upāsaka* (worshipper, propitiator) of the *Brahman* which is *upāsya* (God to be worshipped). As per *Mahopaniṣad*, Parmeśvara (Śiva) is the Supreme *Brahman* (*BrS*, 1-2, 3-8). It is amusing to find that the very *sūtra* which glorifies Nārāyaṇa in *Śrībhāṣya* is interpreted as the glorification of Śiva. For example : *BrS*, 3.2.17.

UPĀSANĀ : MEDITATION

In *BrS*, 4.1.3 :

> *ātmeti tūpaqacchanti grāhayanti ca* ।

Rāmānuja interprets : "God is the self of souls, as souls are the selves of bodies. The *Brahman* that is meditated upon thus retains the difference between the two (*pṛthaktvānusandhānaṁ rakṣitam*)". But Śrīkaṇṭha says "Meditation is to be of the *Brahman* as identical with the self and not as another being. (*Brahma-bhāvenopāsanā-mupāsakasya mukti-karam, anyathā saṁsārānivṛttiḥ* — *BMB,* II, p. 428). This is an obvious tilt to *Advaita*.

IMPORTANCE OF PĀŚUPATA VRATA

In *BrS*, 3.4. 48-49 :

kṛtsnabhāvāt tu gṛhiṇopasaṁhāraḥ ।
maunavad itereṣām apyupadeśāt ।

Śrīkaṇṭha interpretes : The *pāśupata vrata* if practised to the end, leads to liberation. Though this *vrata* is not included in the *āśrama dharma*, the virtues like chastity, control of senses, etc. are associated with this *vrata*.

Śrīkaṇṭha's independent views will be clear in the exposition of his system.

Śivādvaita — Based on Śruti

As contrasted with *KŚ* and *SŚ*, Śrīkaṇṭha takes the *Brahma Sūtra* (*BrS*) as the basic text supporting *Śivādvaita*. To emphasize the supporting *Śruti* to his doctrine, he calls his commentary (*bhāṣya*) on the *BrS* as *Brahma-mīmāṁsā-bhāṣya* (*BMB*) or *Aupaniṣadī mīmāṁsā*. He knew the Āgamic texts and in *BMB* he tries to reconcile *Śruti* and *Āgamas*. He affirms the equality of authority between the two and as Śiva is the author of both *Śruti* and *Āgama*, the difference being that only the upper castes (brāhmaṇa, kṣatriyas and vaiśyas) were eligible to study the former, while the *Āgamas* were open to all.[11]

Like other Śaiva sects, Śrīkaṇṭha builds his system on the three main categories (1) *pati*, (2) *paśu*, (3) *pāśa* or (1) *Śiva*, (2) *jīva*, (3) *mala* or bonds as follows :

PATI : BRAHMA : ŚIVA

The identification of *pati* or the Supreme with Śiva is found even in very early times such as in the *Ṛg Veda,* 10.125.7.

Atharva-śiras Upaniṣad, V. 3 and the *Taittirīya, Āraṇyaka*, XVII.1-5. Śrīkaṇṭha holds that *pati* or *Śiva* characterised by subtle-cum-gross cause-effect of the universe is the *Brahman*.[12] It is beyond the ken of time, space, etc. It is called *bhava* because it exists everywhere at all times. The root √*bhu* connotes 'existence' (*sattā*). *Brahma* being *sad-rūpa* (existential) is called *bhava*.[13] It is called *śarva* as the root √*śṛ* — 'to kill', 'to destroy' implies that it destroys everything at the time of *pralaya*.[14] It is called *Śiva* because it is full of all auspicious attributes and is free from taints.[15] It is the Lord controller of all *jīvas* (*paśus*) and is hence called *paśupati*. (*BMB*, I.127) It causes bondage, birth, maintenance in life, death, *tirobhāva* (restriction of powers of *jīvas*), *anugraha* (grace of granting liberation) — all showing his overlordship (*parameśvaratva*). It dispels all the miseries of the world and is hence designated as *Rudra*.[16] It is called *Mahādeva* as it is engrossed in its own highest bliss (*mahatvena dīvya-mānatayā*). It confers blessings (*śaṁ-*) on all and hence the epithet *śaṁbhu*.

It is *nirguṇa* that is devoid of bad attributes and full of auspicious qualities, — not 'attributeless' as in Śaṅkara. It is bisexual — both He and She.[17]

The above epithets showing identity of *Śiva* (*pati*) and the *Brahman* are acceptable to pure Āgamic sects. Śrīkaṇṭha showed that the Āgamic concepts of Śiva are the same as those of Upaniṣadic *Brahman*.

Like other Śaiva sects, he attributes the five functions (*pañca-kṛtya*) viz. creation, maintenance, destruction of the world and *tirodhāna* and *anugraha* to *Brahman* through his *śaktis*. But like *KŚ* he maintains that 'there is no difference or distinction between the *Brahman* and its powers, (quoted in *BMB*, I. 300-301). Though the *Brahman* is one, there is variety. It consists of both *cid* and *acid* and thereby it recognizes the reality of the world. For the creation of the world, the *Brahman* is both the material and instrumental cause (*BMB*, I. 340-41) the *Brahman*

(Śiva) is neither partial nor cruel. *Jīvas* receive the fruits of their own *karmas* good or evil. When the *jīva*, after experiencing the results of his *karmas* becomes pure-hearted. Śiva favours him with spiritual knowledge and finally *mokṣa* as grace. The concept of grace is as in *Upaniṣads* (e.g. *Kaṭha,* 2.23, *Muṇḍaka,* 3.2.3).

Śrīkaṇṭha does not differ much from *KŚ* and *SŚ* about the concept of *pati* except that he claims Upaniṣadic sanction for the Āgamic concept and adopts the *Viśiṣṭādvaita-vāda* in Śaivism. He has, however, some important differences from Rāmānuja.

PAŚU : JĪVA : INDIVIDUAL SOUL

Śrīkaṇṭha does not believe in the creation or origination of *paśus* or individual souls from Śiva or *Brahman* (*vide supra,* pp. 12-13). The *jīva* has co-status with but **not** identity with *Brahman* as held by Monists.

There have been differences of opinion about the *jīva-Brahma* relationship since pre-*Brahma-sūtra* period. Āśmarathya, a pre-*BrS* thinker, advocates 'difference-cum-non-difference' (*bhedābheda*) between the two (*BrS*, 1.4.16). Auḍulomi, another pre-*BrS* teacher, opines that *Brahman* ensouls *jīva* and functions as his interior ruler. Śrīkaṇṭha holds that the embodiment of the *jīva*, despite this co-status with *Brahman*, is due to some beginningless transgression (*apacāra*) on the part of the *jīva* that the Lord willed to conceal the true nature of the *jīvas*. He points out that the *jīva* is soiled by beginningless *ajñāna* (or *āṇava*), *karma* and *māyā malas*. The soul is forced to enter or leave a body assigned to him for experiencing the fruits of the acts committed by him according to his good or evil predilections. (*BMB,* I, pp. 89-90)

Another view of the *Jīva-Brahma* relation is expressed in the *Kauṣītakī Upaniṣad.*[18]

The relation between *jīvas* and *Brahman* is like that between fire and fiery sparks emanating from the fire. They are of the nature of fire but they are separate and distinct from fire. Śrīkaṇṭha says that this Upaniṣadic analogy simply means that the *jīva* gets 'Name and Form' from the *Brahman*. It does **not** suggest origination or creation of the *jīva* from the Brahmā.

About the problem of Free will of the *jīva*, the *Taittirīya Upaniṣad* firmly declares the Free Will in case of the *jīva* or *vijñāna*[19] (a term used there to designate *jīva*). But Śrīkaṇṭha opines that he is not entirely free. He can undertake some acts of his own free will for the maturation of his *karmas* but it is God who makes him do or refrain from doing it. The position is similar to a boy who can lift a log of wood **with** the help of a strong man. But his actual lifting depends on the will or command of the strong man. (*BMB* on *BrS,* 2.3.41). But, asserts Śrīkaṇṭha, there is no partiality (*vaiṣamya*) or cruelty on the part of God in this matter.[20]

Upaniṣadic statements like *tattvamasi* do not show identity between the *jīva* and the *Brahman*. It is the relation of the pervaded-pervader (*vyāpya-vyāpaka*) type. A log of wood pervaded by fire is called 'fire' though is only a part (*aṁśa*) that is fiery. So the world is pervaded by an *aṁśa* of Maheśvara (*Śvetāśvatara Upanisad,* 4.10). Śrīkaṇṭha concludes : The *jīva* is only an *aṁśa* (particle) of Śiva.[21]

ATOMICITY OF THE JĪVA

If the *jīva* is a part of *Brahman* what is its size. Śrīkaṇṭha states that it is atomic in size but is encased in a *liṅga-śarīra* constituted of the seeds of his future body. He transmigrates to another species with his *liṅga-śarīra* (*BMB,* II, pp. 196-97). Like a lamp illuminating a room of any size, this atomic *jīva* enlivens all the body irrespective of its size (e.g., an ant and an elephant).

MALA : PĀŚA : BONDAGE

Śrīkaṇṭha recognizes four *malas* : *paśutva* (*āṇava*), *karma, māyā,* and *rodha* (*tirodhāna* — concealment). Śrīkaṇṭha does not discuss much about *paśutva* which is the quality of being an individual, due to which the body is regarded identical with soul (*dehātmaikya-bhāva*). He regards *karma* as a beginningless *mala*. Being bound by *karma*—bondage the soul is forced to enter a *māyā* — made body and experiences pleasure or pain. (*BMB,* I, pp. 350-51)

Though both *SŚ* and *Śaiva Viśiṣṭādvaita* flourished in South India and as systems of Śaivism there are naturally many common concepts, the differences between the two systems are important. A few are mentioned below :

As noted above, Śrīkaṇṭha ignores the concept of *āṇava mala*, substitutes it by the concept *paśutva* and accepts a fourth *mala* called *rodha*. The second point noted above is the atomicity of the soul, whereas *SŚ* regards souls as all-pervasive.

Another important difference is about the relation between God and the world. Śrīkaṇṭha regards the world consisting of intelligent (*cit*) and non-intelligent (*a-cit*) as the result of Lord's energy called *cit-śakti* which as intelligence and bliss is **not** different from the Lord. This leads to two conclusion which are unacceptable to *SŚ* viz.

(1) The world is the transformation of the Lord as there is no difference between *śakti* and *śaktimat* (*śakti-śaktimator abhedaḥ*).

(2) Non-intelligent world (bodies, objects of enjoyment etc.) is derived from the same principle as the enjoying soul. (Suryanārāyaṇa Śāstrī, *op. cit.*, p. 20).

Rodha or obscuration is the power of Maheśvara but due to its effect it is regarded as a *pāśa*.[22]

Śrīkaṇṭha regards *karma* as a beginningless and the most powerful bond.

Mokṣa : Liberation

For *mokṣa*, without underestimating the importance of Vedic rites and rituals Śrīkaṇṭha strongly recommends the path of *bhakti* (devotion) consisting of listening to the glory of the Lord, meditation, etc. Thereby the highly merciful Śiva becomes pleased and all the *malas* or bondages are destroyed by His Grace.[23] *Bhakti* was a social force then in the South.

When all the *malas* are washed off, the original Brahma-like qualities or powers of the *jīva* which were so long veiled became manifest — by the Grace of *Parabrahma* — Śiva, the *jīva*'s obscuring bondages are dropped down or eliminated and the real form of *jīva* which is similar to *Brahman* is revealed.[24]

He emphasizes the point that the released soul enjoys Bliss like the *Brahman* but does **not** become merged in the *Brahman* as in *Śāṅkara Vedānta*. The similarity between the two (*jīva* and God) is in the sameness of Bliss.[25] The liberation called *sāyujyatā* is merely similarity in appearance and enjoyment.[26] He is not empowered to carry out the five functions of Śiva such as creation and destruction of the universe, etc.

Śrīkaṇṭha and Siddhānta Śaivism

SŚ authors strongly object to the identity of *māyā* and *cit-śakti*. Thus, Umāpati Śivācārya in the section in '*nimitta-kāraṇa-pariṇām-vādas*' in his work *Sankarpa-nirākaraṇam* refuted this doctrine. Śrīkaṇṭha's non-recognition of an independent origin for the non-intelligent (*acit*) world is tantamount to the *vivarta-vāda* of Śaṅkara. As noted by Sarvajñātma Muni in *Saṅkṣepa-śārīrika*, Vedāntins accept *pariṇāma-vāda* (transformation theory) for empirical purpose but this *pariṇāma-vāda* automatically leads to *vivarta-vāda* :

vyavasthite'smin pariṇāmavāde
samaṁ samāyāti vivarta-vādaḥ.
V. 2

A position repugnant to *SŚ*.

There is a difference of opinion about the nature of *tādātmya* : It means :

(1) One thing appearing as two e.g., *guṇa-guṇin*, substance-attribute.

(2) Two things are so intimately connected as to be regarded as one. This is *Advaita* e.g. *ātmā-paramātmā*.

Śrīkaṇṭha accepts the first view.

Lastly the concept of *jīvan-mukti* (liberation before death, while alive). The *SŚ* believe that to men of mature knowledge, *mokṣa* (liberation) is possible even here (in this world while alive). Śrīkaṇṭha says that even after *brahma-jñāna* one must experience the fruits of his actions during his remaining life-time. These past *karma*s should be eliminated by performing sacrifices, etc. The *mala*s come to an end by the *devayāna* path. And the *Brahman* is attained. Śrīkaṇṭha reconciled Āgamic and Upaniṣadic teachings. He tried to find support for Śaiva theism in the *Vedānta Sūtras*, the reality of the world and the individual, the relative freedom of human will, the essentially ordered nature of the universe that even God respects it. God's greatness is in conferring Grace on deserving individual. The Āgamic doctrine of Śiva's status as a Supreme Being who out of Grace grants liberation and insistence on *bhakti*. This in brief is the permanent contribution of Śrīkaṇṭha.*

---

*For detailed "Estimate" of Śrīkaṇṭha's contribution *vide* S.S. Sūryanārāyaṇa Śāstri's *Śivādvaita of Śrīkaṇṭha,* ch. VII, pp. 230-75.

Notes

1. *kārya-rūpeṇa nānātvam* ।
   abhedaḥ kāraṇātmanā ।
   — *Bhāskara Bhāṣya* (*BrS*, 1-14)
2. S. Radhakrishnan, *The Brahma Sūtra*; Introduction, p. 25. For more details about the theory of *Bhedābheda* see P.N. Śrīnivasācāri's *The Philosophy of Bhedābheda*.
3. *tataḥ samucitam cid-acid-viśiṣṭaḥ parameśvaraḥ kāraṇam ca kāryaṁ ca tat-tad-avasthā-viśeṣāt* ।
   — *BMB* (*Brahma-mīmāṁsa-bhāṣya* — *Śrīkaṇṭha Bhāṣya on BrS* 1-4, 27)
4. *vyāsa-sūtram idam netram viduṣā brahma-darśane* ।
   pūrvācāryaiḥ kaluṣitam śrīkaṇṭhena prasādyate ॥
   — *BMB*, Intro., 5
5. Conclusion by Śaṅkara :
   vedānta-vākya-kusuma-grathanārthatvāt sūtrāṇām ।
   tasmād 'janmādi'-sūtraṁ nānumānopanyāsārth . . . tasya (viz. *yato vā imāni bhūtāni etc.* in *TaittUp*, 3-1) *ca nirṇaya-vākyam* (reconciled with) *ānandād hyevam bhūtāni jāyantīe* । in *TaittUp*, 3.6) — Śaṅkara on *BrS*, 1.1.2 so he states the purpose.
6. *sūkṣma-cid-acid-viśiṣṭam brahma kāraṇam, sthūla-cid-acid viśiṣṭam tat kāryam bhavati* ।
   ato janmādi -lakṣaṇam brahmeti siddhānatḥ ।
   — *BMB* on *BrS*, 1-2, (Vol. I, 135)
7. For an interesting discussion on this topic see *Vedānta-kaustubha* ed. by Dhuṇḍirāj Śāstri, Kashi Sanskrit Series 99, Banaras 1932. An authoritative detailed statement of Roma Chaudhuri's *Doctrine of Nimbārka* but it was not available to me. For a brief yet lucid exposition : *History of Philosophy Eastern and Western*, Vol. I, pp. 338-46.
8. *kārya-kāraṇayor ananyatve'pi kārya-bhūta-cid-acid-prapañcāt kāraṇam atrādhikena śrūyate* ।
   na vayam brahma-prapañcayor atyantam eva bheda-vādinaḥ . . . na vā atyantābheda-vādinah . . na ca bhedābhedavādinaḥ . . kintu śarīra-śarīriṇor iva, guṇa-guṇinoriva ca viśiṣṭādvaita-vādiṇaḥ ।
   —*BMB*, II, p. 231
9. *tataḥ samucitam cid-acid-viśiṣṭaḥ parameśvaraḥ kāraṇam kāryam ca tat-tad-avasthā-viśeṣāt* । — *BMB*, I, p. 57

10. S.S. Śāstri : *Śivādvaita of Śrīkaṇṭha* Appendix IIIA. Resemblance between *Śrībhāṣya* and Śrīkaṇṭha *Bhāṣya*. III B. Resemblance between the *Bhāṣyas* of Śaṅkara and Śrīkaṇṭha.
11. *vayam tu veda-śivāgamayor bhedam na paśyāmaḥ* । *vedo'pi śivāgama iti vyavahāro* । *yuktaḥ, taṣya tat kartṛkatvāt* । *ataḥ śivāgamo dvividhaḥ traivarṇika-viṣayaḥ sarva-viṣyaśceti* । *vedaḥ traivarṇikaviṣayaḥ* । *sarvaviṣayas' cānyaḥ* । *ubhayor eka eva śivaḥ kartā* ।

— *BMB* on *BrS*, 2.2. 38 (*BMB*, II, p. 111)
12. *sthūla-sūkṣma-cid-acid-prapañca-viśiṣṭaḥ parameśvaraḥ kārya-kārana-rūpaḥ* — *BMB*, 1.27 (1. 1.5)
13. *sarvatra sadā bhavatīti bhavaśabda-vācyam* । *bhū-dhātoḥ sattārtha-katvāt* । . . . *tataḥ sadrūpam brahma bhavavācyam bhavati* । — *BMB*, I, 125
14. *śarva-śabdena sṛ-hiṁsāyām iti dhātvarthāt sakala-saṁhartṛ brahma pratipādyate* । — *BMB*, I, 126
15. *anantānanda-kalyāṇa-guṇaika-ghana īśvaraḥ śivaḥ ityucyate* । Also

atyanta-parisuddhātmā — *BMB*, II, 248-49
16. *saṁsāra-rug-drāvakatvāt rudra-śabda-vācyaṁ brahma*

— *BMB*, I, 127
17. *heya-guṇa-rāhityena, kalyāṇa-guṇa sāhityena cobhaya-liṅgaṁ brahma* — *BMB*, II, 248
18. *yathā'gner jvalato visphuliṅgā vipratiṣṭheran, evamevaitasmād*

ātmanaḥ prāṇā yathayatanaṁ vipratiṣṭhante ete.

— *Kauṣitaki BrUp*, 4-20
19. *vijñānam yajñam tanute* ।

karmāṇi tanute'pi ।

TaittUp, 2.5.1
20. *ato jīvakṛta-prayatnā pekṣyatvāt karmasu jīvasya pravartaka iśvaro na vaiṣamyabhāk, tasyāpi svādhīna-pravṛtti-sadbhāvāt vidhi-niṣedhādi vaiyartham na sambhavati* ।

— *BMB*, II, pp. 156-57
21. In concluding *Aṁśādhikaraṇa*, *Śrīkaṇṭha* states :

tato brahmaṇo'mśa-bhūtaḥ jīvas tadaviśavīeṣeṇaika-svabhāva iti yuktam eva । —*BMB, II*, p. 162
22. *rodha-śaktyākhyasya pāśatvavyapadeśasya sivāgameṣu prasiddhatvāt* ।

yadāhuḥ māhesvarī śaktiḥ . . . paranuvarta-nādeva pāśa ityupacaryate । — *BMB*, I, pp. 567-68

23. *tatra śruvaṇa-mananādiniścitasya, bhakti-jñāna-viśeṣābhimukhasya parama-kāruṇikasya mahādeśikasya sarvānūgrāhakasya śivasya para-brahmaṇaḥ prasādātiśayenāsyādhikāriṇaḥ pradhvasta pāśa-paṭalā . . . kaivalya-lakṣmīḥ . . . prayojanaṁ ca bhavati* । —*BMB*, I, 91-95
24. *brahma-prāpta-jīvasya mala tirohitam brahma-sadṛśa guṇa-svarūpaṁ purvaṁ sadeva malāvaraṇāpagamād āvirbhavati . . . sarvānugrāhakasya śivasya parabrahmaṇaḥ prasādena svāvaraṇe male vigalite tat-sadṛśa-guṇam-ātma svarūpaṁ prādurbhavati* । — *BMB*, II, pp. 481-82
25. *yathā brahma sakalān kāmān bhuṅkte tatha mukto'pi, iti bhogasāmya mātram muktasya brahmaṇā, iti samīcīnam* । — *BMB*, II, p. 50 (on *BrS.*, 4.4.21)
26. *brahmaṇā sādṛśyaṁ sāyujyam muktānām, bhogādidharma-sādharmyāt* । —*BMB*, II, p. 501
27. *muktasya parameśvara-sāmye'pi jagad-sṛṣṭyadi-vyāpāra-varjyam asya bhoga-vastuṣu* —*BMB*, II, p. 496

6

Vīra-Śaivism

THE name 'Vīra-Śaivism' applied to this *Śaiva* sect seems to be comparatively recent.* Not only do Śaṅkara and Rāmānuja not mention it, but Śrīpati Paṇḍit (AD 1200), the exponent and the defender of this Āgamic system on the basis of the *Brahmasūtra* (*BrS*) gives the following epithets by which this sect is recognised by others (*kecit*) :

1. *Dvaitādvaita*
2. *Viśeṣādvaita*
3. *Seśvarādvaita*
4. *Śivādvaita*
5. *Sarva-śruti-sāra*
6. *Bhedābheda*
7. *Śakti-viśiṣṭādvaita*

— *Śrīkara Bhāṣya* (*ŚB*) 2.1.5.13, p. 195

The above designations imply some aspects of *Vīraśaiva* philosophy. Śrīpati himself explains how the above synonyms are applicable to the techings of this sect :

---

* According to the archives of the Sanskrit Dictionary Department of the Deccan College Pune, the earliest occurrence of the vocable '*vīra-śaiva*' is in Mādhava's *Śāṅkara Digvijaya* (Dr. Mrs. Yashodhara Wadhvani's letter dated 16.10.1995).

Dvaitādvaita

There is distinction and difference between a river and a sea at the beginning. When the river is yet to join the sea. There is *dvaita* between the two (the river and the sea). When the river joins the sea, it gets merged and becomes identical with the sea. This is *advaita* between the two. Similarly, a devotee (*śaraṇa*) and God (*śaraṇya*, Śiva) are different in the initial stage. Through his devotion, the devotee gets merged into Śiva. This development : merging of difference into non-difference, is implied in the term *dvaitādvaita*.

Viśeṣādvaita

Śrīpati explains this term in different ways:

(i) Śiva is the receptacle of *cit-śakti*. *Cit-śakti* is the supreme cause (*parama kāraṇa*) of the entire *prapañca* or universe. According to Śaivism, *Śakti* is non-different from the Supreme Lord who is both the instrumental as well as the material cause of the universe. This *advaita* has the specially (*viśeṣa*) of *bhedābheda* (difference-cum-non-difference). Hence, it is called *Viśeṣādvaita*. (*ŚB*, II.1.3.17, pp. 135-36)

(ii) Śiva and *jīva* have intelligence or consciousness as the common factor between them. That is they belong to the same **genus**. But the *jīva* is atomic, while Śiva is all-pervading. *Jīva's* knowledge is negligible while Śiva is omniscient. These are the fundamental differences between the two. So the first word in *viśeṣādvaita* viz. *viśeṣa* indicates that sheer *dvaita* (dualism) or mere *advaita* is not proved and is untenable. Hence, the union or *advaita* of the two is the speciality (*viśeṣa*) which is implied in this term.

(iii) Śripati gives a popular etymology of the term as follows:

vi = the *jīva* (Individual Soul)

śeṣa = Omnipresent Śiva

The non-difference [*advaita* between *vi* (Individual Soul) and *śeṣa* (Śiva)] is *viśeṣādvaita*. He pithily puts it as follows:

viś ca śeṣas ca tayoḥ advaitam

This transformation of the *jīva* into Śiva is through constant meditation. (*ŚB*, II, p. 136)

Śeṣvarādvaita

Īśvara or *pati* is the fundamental principle with the potentiality of doing or undoing anything by sheer will-power. This *śakti* (power) is never different or apart from its possessor (*śakti-mat*) or *Īśvara*.

This sect advocates the (ultimate) identity of the *jīva* with *Īśvara* or Śiva. Hence the term *śeṣvarādvaita*.

Śivādvaita

It is **within Śiva** that innumerable varieties of the mobiles and immobiles are created, sustained and dissolved. The universe is **entirely** contained within Śiva. Hence, the universe is non-different from Śiva.

Sarva-Śruti-Sāra

Some *Śruti* texts advocate Monism. Some *Śruti* texts propound Dualism. Both being advocated by *Śruti* are valid. Vīraśaivism advocated 'difference-cum-non-difference' and reconciles the contradiction between the *Śruti* texts. Hence, it is called 'the essence of all *Śrutis*'.

Bhedābheda

Vīraśaivism holds that there is non-difference (*abheda*) in the cause but difference and variety in the effect. For example, the seed of a tree is one but its effects, branches, flowers and fruits are many.

Śakti-viśiṣṭādvaita

As Kumāra Swāmījī explains: Vīraśaivism does not visualise an incurable antinomy between Śiva and Śakti, between being and knowing. It rather effects a synthesis by saying that *Śakti* is the very soul of Śiva: that knowing is inherent in being. There is an integral association between Śiva and Śakti. Hence, this is called *śakti-visiṣṭādvaita*. (*History of Indian Philosophy: Eastern and Western*, p. 398).

Srīpati Paṇḍit does **not** call his philosophy as '**Vīra-Śaivism**'.

Vīra-Śaivism Defined

It is rather curious that popular etymologies of the term '**Vīra-Śaivism**' ignored whether the vowel in *vi* is short or long. They attributed different meanings to *vi-* and *-ra*. In *Siddhānta Śikhāmaṇi* (*SSm*, V. 15-18) we find the following meanings of **Vīraśaivism** — especially of the first term:

1. *Vī* : The lore (*vidyā*) that imparts knowledge of non-difference between Śiva and *jīva.*
2. *Ra*: One who enjoys, indulges in: thus one who enjoys (*ramate*) implicitly in the non-difference between Śiva and *jīva* is a *Vīraśaiva*.[1]

The same author now regards that *Vīraśaiva* is the correct term and defines:

Vī — *vidyā* 'knowledge born', i.e., derived from *Vedānta*

Ra — *ramate* — one who enjoys (is interested in).[2] The *Parameśvara Tantra* (*paṭala* 9.1.15) gives a number of such etymologies such as:

"Hero-ship" (*vīratva*) is the dauntless action of a brave man in a battle. He who is firm (in faith) by his excellent devotion and non-attachment (*vairāgya*) is a *Vīraśaivsa*.[3]

From the various definitions of 'Vīraśaivism' and the usage of applying the epithet *vīra* (a hero, a warrior), I think *vīra* in *Vīra-Śaiva* means 'a staunch follower of Śaivism', we find the use of the term *Vīra Vaiṣṇava* in Tamil Nadu and *Vaiṣṇava Vīra* in Maharashtra : implying 'a steadfast or firm devotee of Viṣṇu'. But it does not indicate a particular school of philosophy. The synonyms used by Śrīpati Paṇḍit are philosophically more significant.

The "Prophet"(s) of Vīraśaivism

There are two views among *Vīra-Śaivas* as to the founders of their sect. Some regard Bāsava as a 'founder' or 'prophet' of Vīraśaivism. Bāsava was a brāhmaṇa from Bagewadi. Dist. Bījāpur, Karnataka. He was not merely a mystic or a religious man but a revolutionary social reformer. He advocated equality of status to women, abolition of caste system, dignity of labour and such other advanced views in those days. He tried to breathe new spirit in a decaying society. His *vacanas* (sayings) express his intense devotion to *kūḍala saṅgama-deva* (Śiva). They remind us of similar earnest devotion to Śiva in the Tamil songs of *Tevāram* and *Abhaṅgas* of Marāṭhā saints.

In AD 1160 Bāsava established *Śūnya siṁhāsana* at Kalyāṇī in Bidār District of Karnataka. It was a forum — a meeting place for contemporary saints and mystics like Channa Bāsava, Alam Prabhu, the great lady saint Akkā Mahādevī and others. For the moral and spiritual uplift of the masses, the *vacanas* of these saints serve a beacon light. There is no differences of opinion that these *vacanas* form an invaluable contribution to Kannaḍa literature. But Bāsava did **not** write a systematic treatise on Vīra-Śaivism. It is from his *vacanas* that we find that as an ardent devotee he believed in the efficacy of the name of Kūḍala-Saṅgama-deva (*Bhaktasthala Vacana,* No. 167, p. 115). His visualization of *Śiva-liṅga* as 'more brilliant than a thousand suns, incomprehensible yet blissful which renders him speechless' (*Māheśvarasthala*, No. 183, p. 396). *Aikyasthala*, Nos. 34-35, p. 540), certainly show that he was a great mystic, saint. He was a religious organizer and a social reformer. M.R. Sakhare (*History and Philosophy of Lingayat Religion*, pp. 426-27). Kumāraswāmījī (in *History of Philosophy — Eastern and Western*, p. 395) give the credit of founding Vīraśaivism to Bāsava for "assiduous and impartial historical research" of Kannaḍa scholars have proved beyond doubt that these so-called *ācāryas* are not the originators of *Vīra-Śaiva* faith (*op.cit.*, p. 398).

Five Ācāryas : Real Founders

There is another school among *Vīra-Śaivas* which regards the following pre-Bāsava teacher-saints as the founders of this faith. They are : 1. Revaṇasiddha, 2. Maruḷasiddha, 3. Ekorāma, 4. Paṇḍitārādhya, 5. Viśvārādhya. They are believed to have been born out of the following *Śiva-liṅgas*.

(1) Revaṇasiddha : *Someśa liṅga* at Kollipak

(2) Maruḷasiddha : *Siddheśa liṅga* at Ujjain, Dist. Bellari, Karnataka.

(3) Ekorāma : *Śrisailya Mallikārjuna*, Kurnool Dist. Andhra Pradesh.

(4) Paṇḍitārādhya : *Rāmanātha liṅga* at Kedārnāth (Uttar Pradesh).

(5) Viśvārādhya : *Viśveśvara liṅga* at Vārāṇasī (Uttar Pradesh).

This school regards Bāsava as a social and religious reformer and **not** the founder of this sect.

In their enthusiasm to proclaim the antiquity of their

sect, blind followers of these *ācāryas* have blown up their greatness out of proportion and exiled them from historicity to mythology. Thus Revaṇasiddha, the first *ācārya* had founded a *maṭh* at Bale-Honnur, in Chikkamanglur District of Karnataka. The *maṭh* exists today. But the blind followers relegated him to *tretā yuga*, attributing to him the supervision of the worship of thirty million *liṅgas* simultaneously for Vibhīṣaṇa, the brother of Rāvaṇa. Such accounts naturally evoked sharp reprisal from modern scholars like M.R. Sakhare, Kumāraswāmījī and others. S.C. Nandimath who is a strong advocate of these pre-Bāsava *ācāryas* as the founders of Vīraśaivism, ruefully admits:

> The five Ārādhyas (Ācāryas) are the founders of Vīraśaivism according to tradition. But unfortunately no authoritative historical information about them had been made available as yet. —*Handbook of Vīraśaivism* p. 18.

In this context, a historical convulsion in pre-Bāsava period is worth noting. Towards the end of the tenth century AD, Muslim aggression in North India destroyed the holy places of Somanāth (Saurāṣṭra) and Mathurā. Both were centres of the *Pāśupata* sect. The *Pāśupata* teachers fled to the South and Kings in Karnataka and Andhra generously supported these refugees as is seen from the inscriptions from the eleventh to thirteenth century AD. At that time brāhmaṇa followers of Vasugupta also left Kaśmīr and settled in Mahārāṣṭra and Karnataka. As Gunaratna, the Jain commentator of Haribhadra's *Ṣaḍ-darśana samuccaya* informs us that these *Pāśupata* brāhmaṇas, besmeared themselves with holy ashes, worshipped the *liṅga* forms of Śiva, wore a *liṅga* on their persons in addition to *yajñopavīta* (sacred thread). Practices adopted by *Vīra-Śaivas*. Kannaḍa inscriptions in Bījāpur district (of AD 1074-75, 1147, 1158) state that these *Pāśupata* brāhmaṇas were not only expert in the *Pāśupata Sūtra* but also in *Vedas*, *Śāstras*, *Itihāsa* and *Purāṇas* and in Yogic practice as well. In their *maṭhas* attached to their *liṅga* temples, they taught this to **all** irrespective of castes and communities. This cosmopolitanism was later adopted by Bāsava and his followers. The *Pāśupata* centres of these brāhmaṇas, their temples such as those of Kedāreśvara, Pañcaliṅga, Somanāth Huli (Dist. Belgaum) are now inherited by *Vīra-Śaivas*. Their formative influence on Vīra-Śaivism is noted by S.C. Nandimath (*op.cit.*, pp. 8-10).

Vīra-Śaiva Philosophy

A systematic presentation of *Vīra-Śaiva* philosophy in pre-Bāsava period is found in Śrīpati Paṇḍit's *Śrīkara Bhāṣya*, a commentary on the *Brahma Sūtra* (*BrS*). Śrīpati was a brāhmaṇa of Vijayavāṭikā (Bezwada) in Andhra Pradesh. He wrote a lucid commentary on the *BrS*, and has shown that the *āgama*-based faith, viz. Vīra-Śaivism has full support of the Brāhmaṇical *prasthāna*, the *Brahma Sūtra* (*BrS*).

After paying respects to his *guru-paraṁparā* (tradition of teachers) from Śiva to Ekorāma, he states that his *Bhāṣya* called *Śrīkara* contains the essence of Vyāsa's *BrS*. It is an ornament (authentic presentation) of *Viśeṣādvaita* philosophy. It is a synthesis of *Vedas*, *Upaniṣads* and *Āgamas*. This *Bhāṣya* is like a wish-yielding tree to *Mokṣa*-seeking *Śaivas* and pure *Vaidikas*.[4]

As stated at the beginning of this chapter. Śrīpati gives the following names of his *Bhāṣya*, each indicating the nature of its philosophy:

(1) *Dvaitādvaita*,

(2) *Viśiṣṭādvaita*,

(3) *Seśvarādvaita*

(4) *Śivādvaita*,

(5) *Sarva-śruti-sāra*,

(6) *Bhedābheda*

(7) *Śakti-Viśiṣṭādvaita*

All these terms are explained above.

Pati : Para-Śiva : Brahma : Liṅga

As with other *Śaiva* sects, *Vīra-Śaivas* regard Śiva as the Supreme Principle who controls both *Paśu* and *Pāśa*. His speciality is that he is a synthesis or rather receptacle of contradictory characteristics such as *sat* (manifest), *asat* (non-manifest), 'embodied'-'disembodied', 'with characteristics', 'without characteristics'. Commenting on *BrS*, 1.1.2 Śrīpati adopts the term *Brahman* for *Pati* which is characterised by five functions viz. creation, maintenance and annihilation of the universe, concealment (*tirodhāna*) and grace (*anugraha*).[5]

Śrīpati explains the relation between the world and the Lord as: the Lord is the cause and the world, effects. Pots are created from clay, that means they are clay before creation and even after destructions, are clay. In commenting on *asad-vyapadeśān* etc. (*BrS*, 2.1.17) he says:

> Before creation the world was in a subtle stage (*sūkṣma*) and was hence called *asat* : after creation, a gross stage — it was called *sat*. Just as a tortoise spreads out its feet, *Parama* Śiva manifests out of himself, the world characterised by name and form. And just as a tortoise withdraws its legs within itself, the Lord conceals within Himself the universe. (*ŚB*, II, p. 198 on *BrS*, 2.1.18)

On *BrS,* 2.1.20 (*ŚB*, II, p. 198) he explains the same by taking an example of a *yogī* who controls his breath at the time of entering into *samādhi*, exhales it (and breathes normally) after the *samādhi* period. Similarly the Lord extends the universe at the time of creation and withdraws it within at the time of *pralaya*.

He concludes the section by stating that hereby the topic of the difference between the world and the Lord, and the *mithyātva* of the world are disproved and the doctrine of difference-cum-non-difference is vindicated (*ŚB*, II, p. 198). In other words the world is real and eternal.

Though the relation between *jīva* (individual soul) and God is like that of the body and the embodied (i.e., the *ātman*), God is eternally free. All things (worlds) are accommodated in *ākāśa* (the sky) but it is free from all blemishes, etc. of those worlds contained within it. The Supreme Śiva, though the cause of everything and immanent in everything is untouched by their blemishes.[6]

The Supreme Śiva is independent. As his body is not *kārmika* (formed out of the result of *karma*s) pleasure-pain, etc. do not affect him. *Jīva*s (individual souls) are seen to experience miseries, etc. due to their beginningless *karma-mala*, there is neither partially or cruelty on the part of Śiva in alotting them pleasure or pain.[7]

On the contrary, by conferring grace on *jīva*s. He removes the beginningless *mala* and absorbs the *jīva* within himself. Due to beginningless *mala*, the *jīva* (individual soul) and Śiva are at first separate but like rivers merging into the sea, the *paśu* or *jīva* becomes one with Śiva. Attainment of such a state is the culmination of spiritual experience.

Liṅga : Brahman

Although Śrīpati showed how Vīra-Śaivism has Upaniṣadic basis and as such it is a Vedic sect, it is mainly based on

Āgamas which regard *liṅga* as the highest principle. *Vīra-Śaivas* call themselves *Liṅgāyats*. The concept of *liṅga* is already discussed in *supra* (pp. 20-24) where it was shown that what *Vedāntins* call the *Brahman*, the Śaivites call it *Pati* and *Liṅga*. *Vīra-Śaiva* texts state the *liṅga* concept as follows:

> That from which the universe comes out (is evolved) and that in which it is dissolved (is withdrawn) that is the *Liṅga* — the eternal Brahman.[8] (*SSn*, VI.37) The *Candra-jñānāgama* (*Kriyāpāda* 3.8) goes a step further and asserts that the creation and dissolution of the universe takes place *in the Brahman which is called Liṅga.*[9]

The same has been emphasized in the *Vedāntasāra-Vīraśaiva Cintāmaṇi* which quotes *TaitUp* (3.1.1) and says that 'the *Brahman* is the cause of the creation and dissolution of the universe (*Layāgamana-Kāraṇam*) — an echo of the term *Tajjalān* in the *ChāUp* (3.14.1).

The term *liṅga* is derived from two Sanskrit roots $\sqrt{l\bar{\imath}}$ — 'to dissolve', $\sqrt{ga}$ or $\sqrt{ga\dot{m}}$ — 'to go forth'. *Śivānubhava Sūtra* (3.3) defines : "*Liṅga* is that in which the mobile and the immobile universe merges and from which it (i.e., the universe) issues forth (evolved)[10] — an echo from *Sūkṣmāgama* (*Kriyāpāda* 6.6).

Śiva-Liṅga is not merely the upper protruding part but includes its base (*pīṭha*). These are respectively called Śiva and Śakti, *prakāśa* and *vimarśa* (Śiva's inherent powers of knowledge and action), *nāda* and *bindu* (both esoteric untranslatable) terms (*Candrajñānāgama, Kriyāpāda paṭala* 3.13).[12] The axiomatic belief of *Śaivas* is that the above pairs (Śiva-Śakti) constitute one whole and inherently inseparable thus echoing *Kaṭha* (2.5.15), *Muṇḍaka* (2.2.9) *Upaniṣads* and *BG*, XIII.17, *Sūkṣmāgama* (*Kriyāpāda, paṭala* 6.9) says that the sun, the moon, stars and other luminaries shine by his (*liṅga*'s) illumination.[13]

In short, the icon of stone, crystal, etc., which a *Vīra-Śaiva* receives from his *guru* at the time of initiation is the symbol of *parabrahman*, the Supreme Lord. Both men and women are eligible to wear it. The *liṅga* is never to be separated from the person of the initiated. The initiated person has to perform the worship of the *liṅga* assiduously everyday. Śrīpati Paṇḍit asserts that *liṅga-dhāraṇa* is sanctioned like the acceptance of Agnihotra.[14] After *liṅga-dhāraṇa* no impurity from birth and death (*sūtaka*) or that of menstruation (in the case of women) needs be observed. This *liṅga* which is given by the *guru* is called *īṣṭa-liṅga*.

Classification of Liṅgas

Liṅgas are mainly classified according to their spiritual significance: 1. *īṣṭa,* 2. *prāṇa,* 3. *bhāva.* They are called *sthūla, sūkṣma, parātpara* by Reṇukācārya (*SSn,* 6.2.8). *Liṅga* is also called *sthala* as it is the Absolute *Para-brahman* characterised by *sat,* (real existence), *cit* and *ānanda* (bliss) and is the receptable of all beings (*Śivānubhava Sūtra,* 2.8).

Prāṇa-Liṅga

SŚn (12-67) describes *Prāṇa-liṅga* as follows:[15]

> When the aspirant (*sādhaka*) performs *prāṇāyāma* as per *guru's* guidance, light emanates from the yogic plexus *Mūlādhāracakra*. It proceeds upwards and rests in the plexus called *anāhatacakra* which is located in the heart region. This spiritual light illuminating the heart is called *Prāṇa-liṅga*. This is the resting place (*sthala*) of *prāṇa*. It being formless, can be grasped only mentally.

Bhāva-Liṅga

The Supreme soul in the eight-petalled lotus (plexus) in the heart (region) is in the form of *prāṇa* but the soul abides in the thousand-petalled lotus in the brain-region wherein both *kriyā* (action) and *bhāva* (feeling or thinking) get dissolved. It is to be propitiated by the feeling or thinking one self being Śiva Himself (*śivo'ham*). Where this feeling or thought too is lost — that *sthala* is *Bhāvaliṅga*. It is connected with *ātman* and should be approached through *bhakti*, *iṣṭa-liṅga*, *prāṇa-liṅga* and *bhāva-liṅga* are the *āvaraṇas* (protective coverings) of the gross, subtle and *kāraṇa* bodies — *sthūla* (gross, physical), *sūkṣma* (subtle) and *kāraṇa śarīras*, respectively.

There are six *liṅgas* corresponding to six *sthalas* (summarised from S.N. Dasgupta — *History of Indian Philosophy*, V.62-63) (*ṣaṭ-sthalas*)—*sthala* a resting place.

1. *Māhātma-liṅga*: It is subtle, without beginning and end, self-sufficient, indefinable, graspable by intuition of the heart.
2. *Prasāda-ghana-liṅga* — *Sādākhya tattva*: It is beyond sense-perception. It contains seeds of consciousness.
3. *Cara-liṅga*: The pure luminous *puruṣa* without inside and outside and formless. It is known as *ātman*.
4. *Śiva-liṅga*: The ego as manifested by *icchā-śakti* (Śiva's will-power).
5. *Guru-liṅga*: This *shtala* by its own knowledge and powers functions as a *guru*.
6. *Ācāra-liṅga*: It upholds the universe and holds them all in the mind.

There are many other classifications of *liṅga* but the important ones and those associated with *ṣaṭ-sthala* are noted here.

Vīraśaivism advocates the path or *bhakti* for Śiva (self)-realization.

Paśu : Ātmā : Piṇḍa

Vīra-Śaivas use the following terms to denote individual soul (*jīva*): *aṇu, ātmā, jīva, paśu, pudgala, kṣetrajña, puruṣa.*

Many of these terms are current from Upaniṣadic time and the rest in other *Śaiva* sects *Vīra-Śaivas* use two special terms to indicate the spiritual progress of the *jīva* viz. *piṇḍa* and *aṅga.*

Piṇḍa is the individual soul who has a pure heart, has his 'cage' of sins broken and whose present birth is the last birth.[16] According to the 'body' of the *piṇḍa*, it is classified as (1) *sthūla piṇḍa* (gross-body), (2) *sūkṣma piṇḍa* (subtle-body or *liṅga-śarīra*), (3) *kāraṇa piṇḍa* (pertaining to *kāraṇa* body or *kāraṇa śarīra*).

Aṅga is derived (in the medieaval fashion) as follows :

aṁ — the *Brahman*, $\sqrt{ga}$ — *gacchati* : 'goes'.

The individual soul that strives to reach the *Brahman* is called *aṅga.*[17] They interpret the Upaniṣadic *mahāvākya* : *tattvam asi* as follows :

tat	—	*liṅga* or Supreme Soul
tvam	—	*aṅga* as explained above
asi	—	*tādātmya* 'one-ness, identity'

The *mahāvākya* means *liṅgāṅga-saṁyoga* (the union of *liṅga* and *aṅga*) or *liṅgāṅga-sāmarasya* (merging or union of *liṅga* and *aṅga* (these terms are explained above).

Śrīpati Paṇḍit enumerates the general characteristics of a *jīva* as compared with those of Śiva. He says that there are four types of liberation (*mukti*) viz.:

(1) *Salokatā* (residence in Lord's, i.e., Śiva's, region)

(2) *Samīpatā* (vicinity to Śiva)

(3) *Sarūpatā* (similarity with Śiva's appearance)

(4) *Sāyujyatā* (total identity with Śiva : merger in Śiva)

These four types of liberation are possible as *jīva* and Śiva, though bracketed in a common **genus** are different in **species** in their size, knowledge etc. (*ŚB*, II, p. 201). The relation between Śiva and *jīva* is like that between the fire and its sparks. (*ŚB* on *BrS*, 2.3.17 an Upaniṣadic concept).

Jīvas are many and eternal. But it is by way of sport that the Supreme Śiva or *mahāliṅga* assumes *upādhis* or *malas* and re-assumes Śivahood by washing off *malas*. In other words, a *jīva* with *malas* washed off becomes automatically Śiva and just as milk mixed with milk or *ghī* with *ghī* or oil with oil gets merged with no distinction (between the two) so *jīvas* get merged in Śiva.[18] This is obviously an echo (nay practically a quotation) from the *Ātmopaniṣad*, 22, 23 *Vira-Śaivas* use different terms like *liṅga*, *sthala* but they use Upaniṣadic terms like *viśva taijasa*, *prājña* to denote the stages of the *ātman* (*MāṇḍūkyaUp*, 3, 4, 5) as in *Śivānubhava Sūtra*, 5.61 (Quoted in *E.V.*, p. 40).

There is not much discussion on *mala* in *ŚB* but *Vīra-Śaivas*, like other *Śaiva* sects, believe that *jīva*'s original Śiva-like powers become limited but the *jīva* regains them in full, when the *malas* are cleansed completely.

Evolution of the Universe (Tattvas)

Like other sects of Śaivism like *KŚ, SŚ*, *Vīra-Śaivas* believe in thirty-six *tattvas* in a somewhat different terminology.

At the beginning (before the creation of the universe) there was only Śiva or *niṣkala-liṅga*. This *parabrahman* called Śiva desired to create the universe 'for obliging *yogīs*' (*yoginām upakārāya*) as *Sūkṣmāgama* (*Kriyāpāda*, 1.18.19) puts it.

According to one classification, the *tattvas* are classified

in three categories — (1) *Śuddhādhva* (pure path?), (2) *Miśrādhva* (mixed path), (3) *Aśuddhādhva* (impure path).

(1) The *tattvas* in *Śuddhādhva* are :

1. *śiva*, 2. *śakti*, 3. *sadāśiva*, 4. *īśvara* and 5. *śuddha vidyā*.

The above principles are said to be related to *prasāda-liṅga, cara-liṅga, śiva-liṅga, guru-liṅga* and *ācāra-liṅga*.

(2) *Miśrādhva*: The following *tattvas* are included herein:

1. *māyā*, 2. *kāla*, 3. *kalā*, 4. *vidyā*, 5. *niyati*, 6. *rāga* and 7. *puruṣa*

(3) *Aśuddhādhva* contains the following twenty-four *tattvas* corresponding to *Sāṅkhya tattvas*:

Twenty-four Tattvas (Details)

1-4 (1) *prakṛti*, (2) *buddhi* (intelligence), (3) *ahaṁkāra* (ego), (4) *manas* (mind).

5-9 Cognitive sense-organs of : (5) Audition — ears, (6) Touch (i.e., skin), (7) Vision (eyes), (8) Taste (tongue), (9) Smell (nose).

10-14 Conative sense-organs, viz.: (10) *vāk* — speech, (11) Hands (action), (12) Feet (Locomotion), (13) Organ of urination, (14) and of excretion.

15-19 *tanmātras* : (15) *śabda* (sound), (16) *sparśa* (touch), (17) *rūpa* (form), (18) *rasa* (taste), (19) *gandha* (smell).

20-24 *Mahābhūtas* — gross elements : (20) *ākāśa* (ether), (21) *vāyu* (wind), (22) *tejas* (fire), (23) *jala* (water), (24) *pṛthvī* (earth).

Another enumeration of these *tattvas* is given in *Parameśvarāgama* (2.17.29-33).[19] According to another classification the group of twenty-five (*Sāṁkhya*) *tattvas* the *ātma-tattvas* or *aṅga tattvas* and the *liṅga tattvas* include (five) *śaktis*, or *kalā*, (five) *sādākhya* and *śiva tattva* or *mahāliṅga*.

Though there is a difference in terminology, Kāśmir Śaivism, *Siddhānta* Śaivism and *Vīra* Śaivism (and *Śāktas* as well) recognize 36 *tattvas* out of which the first twelve are esoteric and the next twenty-four are those of *Sāṁkhyas*. All these *tattvas* are evolved out of the *śakti* — the will power of Śiva.

Vīra-Śaivism has *ṣaṭ sthalas* correspondence between *sthala, śakti-pāta*, or *āvirbhāva* is given below:

Sthala		*Āvirbhāva of Śakti-pāta*
1. *Bhakta*	—	*Māheśvara-Tattvāvirbhāva*
2. *Māheśvara*	—	*Sadāśiva-tattvasākṣātkāra*
3. *Prasādī*	—	*Siva-śakti-saṁyoga*
4. *Prāṇa-liṅga*	—	*Sarva-bhuvana-gamana-parokṣa-darśana*
5. *Śaraṇa*	—	*Aṇimādi-aiśvarya saṁpannatā*
6. *Aikya*	—	*Unmanī-avasthā prāpti*

(*Explanation follows*)

A few details of each stage will show how the *jīva* (individual soul), originally different from Śiva, progresses step-by-step till he merges (becomes identical with *aikya*) in Śiva.

1. *Bhakta-sthala* : Śrīpati recommends the listening (to the glory of Śiva or Śiva's names, constant meditation of *Āgama* and *Vedānta* which explains the relation of body

and spirit (*jīva*) and universal spirit (*śiva*). One should realize that *parama* Śiva is eternal and Supreme Bliss.

For the above realization *bhakti* (devotion to Śiva) is essential. Hence it is called *bhakta-sthala*. S.C. Nadiamath (*op.cit.*, pp. 168-69) gives the following features of the *bhakta-sthala*:

(1) Firm belief and devotion to Śiva only. No other god should be worshipped.

(2) The *Iṣṭa-liṅga* offered by the *guru* at the time of initiation is the symbol of the Supreme Śiva.

(3) To lead a chaste moral life.

(4) Belief in the distinctness of the *jīva* (individual soul) and Śiva (the Supreme Reality) to be observed.

2. *Māheśvara-sthala*: All the features of the *bhakta-sthala* are to be observed more minutely and scrupulously. In addition to these, emphasis is on observance of holy vows (*vrata*s and *niyama*s).

Śrīpati uses the term *sadāśiva* in the sense of 'Supreme Śiva' (***vide ŚB***, II, p. 73 on *BrS*, 1.1.21) where *Hiraṇmaya-Puruṣa* is called Sadāśiva. It may be noted that Śrīkaṇṭha identifies 'the golden person within the sun' with Śiva.

Śrīpati insists on the realization of this *Sadāśiva-tattva* by observance of holy vows and meditation.

3. *Prasādi-sthala*: Śrīpati states that following the *Śiva-yoga*, brings about the union of Śiva-Śakti at *brahmarandhra* (cerebral apperture). This is the real *prasāda* or grace of Śiva and the person so blessed is *prasādī*.

Nandimath (*op.cit.*, p. 171) emphasizes only desireless action (*niṣkāma-karma*) in this stage.

In these first three states. *Kriyā* (action) is emphasized. But the duality between the *jīva* and Śiva still remains. In the next three stages, spiritual knowledge is emphasized and the distinction between *jīva* and *śiva* gradually disappears. Ultimately there is complete merger and identity of the *jīva* and *śiva* in the last *aikya* stage.

4. *Prāṇa-liṅga-sthala*: Śrīpati says that the *guru* enters the person of the disciple and helps him to move through all yogic *cakras* and makes him directly perceive all *bhuvanas* like Śiva.

S.C. Nandimath (*op.cit.*, p. 172) equates *prāṇa* with *ātman*. The Self is looked upon as *liṅga*. The visualization of the internal light of *prāṇa* or *ātman* is achieved by *Śiva-yoga*. This stage is presided over by *jaṅgama liṅga*.

5. *Śaraṇa-sthala*: Śrīpati says that at this stage, the *jīva* attains all spiritual powers like *aṇimā*, *laghimā*, etc. S.C. Nandimath (*op.cit.*, pp. 172-73) says: At this stage *bhakti* develops into complete self-surrender (*prapatti*). The duality between the *jīva* and Śiva is very thin. It has practically vanished.

6. *Aikya-sthala*: At this stage, the *jīva* ceases to exist as distinct and different from Śiva. There is a complete unqualified identity between the Soul and the Deity. S.C. Nandimath (*op.cit.*, pp. 173-74) says that *vacana-śāstra* tends to *advaita* — Śrīpati says that this is the *jīvan-mukti* (liberation during life-time) stage.

This is the *sādhanā-mārga* to *mokṣa*.

Mokṣa (Liberation)

We have seen that *mokṣa* (liberation from bonds of *saṁsāra*) is looked upon as the highest achievement (*parama puruṣārtha*) in life, according to all schools of Indian Philosophy except the materialists (*supra*, pp. 15-16). Śaivism holds that *mokṣa* is liberation from three types of bonds or *malas* viz. *āṇava*, *karma*, and *māyīya*. Vīra-Śaivism has prescribed *dīkṣā* (initiation into the *Śaiva* spiritual path) as the condition precedent for all aspirants to *mokṣa*. As *Siddhānta Śikhāmani* (*SŚn*) states: "By *dīkṣā* three types of *malas* disappear and knowledge about Lord Śiva is imparted".[20]

Śrīpati asserts that 'by the knowledge about God one gets release from all bonds'. By the knowledge of the *Brhman* called Śiva, there is liberation from the bonds of *māyā* consisting of three *malas*. By realization (vision of Śiva) one attains the Supreme *Śiva-tattva* (the attainment being the gain of the highest object of human beings.[21] But Śrīpati assures that even by *bhakti* (devotion to Śiva) one can achieve the four types of liberation (such as *salokatā*, *samīpatā*, *sarūpatā* and *sāyujyatā*).[22]

Śiva-yogī Śivācārya in *SŚn* says that mere spiritual knowledge is not enough. It should be reinforced by *bhakti* and be assimilated by meditation on the knowledge imparted. *Bhāva* (emotional attachment) is essential both for *bhakti* and *jñāna*. *SŚn* makes an emphatic statement:

> Even a *yogī* without *bhāva* can never be able to visualize Śiva.[23]

Like all other *Śaiva* sects, *Vīra-Śaivas* believe that it is only due to Śiva's grace that one can get liberated.

There is a social aspect and personal restraint also on those who deem to have realized Śiva that every *Śiva-yogī* must follow the daily prescribed routine of *karmas*. As *SŚn* (16-4-9) states:

> Even a desireless *Mahāyogī* should not give up the routine religious duties.[24]

This is necessary to retain discipline in the followers and for their own guidance. This is *bhakti-karma-samuccaya* according to Vīra-Śaivas. Dr. Candra Śekhara Śivācārya (in *Siddhānta Śikhāmaṇi-samīkṣā*) notes: '*Karma* associated with *bhāvanā* is *bhakti* and *bhāvanā* associated with *jñāna* is meditation (*Nididhyāsana*)'. The objection that such a *yogī* should by doing a *karma* must experience the fruit, is not correct. It is not applicable to him as he is *jīvan-mukta* (liberated while alive). Śrīpati says that a *jīvan-mukta* realizes that Śiva is in everything (*sarva-śivātmaka-jñāna-sadbhāva*). If at all, he has a very tenuous relation with his mind (*antaḥkaraṇa*). The realization that he is the *Brahman* (*ahaṁ brahmāsmi*), he is always absorbed in the experience of *Brahma*-hood He is not affected by the results of these *karmas* — if affected at all, it will be 'like the light of camphor as against blazing light of midday sun' as they have realized that everything is Śiva.[25]

What is the condition of the *jīvan-mukta* or a person who has realized Śiva, after the fall of his body (death)? He loses his individuality and merges into (becomes identical with) Śiva. This is also the view of *advaita* advocated by Śaṅkara. This however does not mean that *Vīra-Saiva* accepts the Śaṅkara's view about the unreality (*mithyātva*) of the world. As Śiva is real, his creation, the world is real. This automatically discards the *adhyāsa-vāda* of Śaṅkara. Respectful non-controversiality is a special feature of Vīra-Śaivism. As the *SŚn* (*Siddhānta-Śikhāmaṇi*) states. *Veda*, *Sāṁkhya*, *Yoga*, *Pāñcarātra* and *Pāśupata* are respectable. They should not be controverted by arguments (against them).[26]

APPENDIX

Guidelines to Vīra-Śaivas

According to *Candra-jñānāgama*[27] (*Kriyāpāda* 9-4) the following duties are prescribed for every *Vīra-Śaiva*:

1. *Liṅgācāra* (*liṅga*-worship)
2. *Sadācāra* (Good behaviour or conduct)
3. *Śivācāra* (Unflinching faith only in Śiva)
4. *Gaṇācāra* (Behaviour like fraternity viz. not to listen to

derogation of Lord Śiva, Vīra-Śaivism.

5. *Bhṛtyācāra* (Service to devotees of Śiva).

1. *Liṅgācāra* includes daily worship of the *liṅga* given by the *guru*, mental concentration on it and profound and repeated meditation on it.
2. *Sadācāra*: Literally, the conduct of the good. Here to behave like a pious *Śiva-bhakta* and to serve the *guru*, *jaṅgamas* with money earned by honest means.[28]
3. *Sivācāra*: Firm faith that Śiva is the Supreme *Brahman*. There is no other resort (*Candra-jñānāgama, Kriyāpāda* 9.7).
4. *Gaṇācāra*: Explained above.
5. *Bhṛtyācāra*: To regard *Śiva-Yogī* as Śiva himself and to render services to him like unto a master (*Siddhānta Śikhāmaṇi*, 9.9).[29]

Notes

1. *vīra-śabdenocyate vidyā śiva-jīvaikya-bodhikā* ।
   tasyām ramante ye śaivā vīra-śaivās tu te matāḥ ॥
   — *Siddhānta-Śikhāmaṇi* (*SŚn*). V. 16
2. *vedānta-janyam yaj jñānam vidyeti pari-kīrtyate* ।
   vidyāyām ramate tasyām vīra ityabhidhīyate ॥
   — *SŚn*, V. 18
3. *vīratvam nāma deveśī yathā vīro raṇe bhaṭaḥ* ।
   tathā mate ca sad-bhaktyā vīro vairāgyato dṛḍhāt ॥
   — *Pārameśvara Tantra* 9-1 Quoted by Aḷḷi in *SŚn*
4. *śrī-vaiyyāsika-brahma-sūtra-pada-mukhyārtham śivānu-grahāt* ।
   bhāṣyaṁ 'śrīkara'-nāmakam śrīmacchrīpati-paṇḍitendra-yatinā vyācakṣate sāmpratam ॥
   aśeṣopaniṣat-sāra-viśeṣādvaitamaṇḍanam ।
   śiva-jñāna-pradam sūtra-bhāṣyam jayatu sarvadā ॥12॥
   vedāgamārtha-tattvajña-śaivānām mokṣa-kāṅkṣiṇām ।
   vaidikānām viśuddhānām etad bhāṣyam tu kalpakam ॥13॥
   — *Śrīkara Bhāṣya* (*SB*), p. 2
5. *janmādi-sṛṣṭi-sthiti-vilaya tirodhānātmakaṁ kṛtya-pañcakam*

asya cidacit-prapañca-vilāsasya ।

— *SB* II, p. 29

6. *tathā parameśvaraḥ sarva-kāraṇatva-sarva-śarīratva sarvāntaryāmitvena vyavasthito'pi sarva-doṣa-kalaṅka-vilakṣaṇaḥ* ।

— *SB* II, p. 194

7. *loke jīvānām sukha-duḥkha-bhoga-darśanāt parameśvarasya vaiṣamya-nairghṛṇyādi-prasaktitṛnopapadyate* । *sāpekṣatvāt jīva-kṛta-puṇya-pāpa-sāpekṣatvāt* ।

— *SB*, II, p. 208 on *BrS*, 2.1.11.34

8. *layaṁ gacchati yatraiva jagadetaccarācaram* ।
punaḥ punaḥ samutpattim tal-liṅgam brahma śāśvatam ।

— *Siddhānta Śikhāmaṇi-Liṅgadhāraṇa*, 16

9. *jaṭhare līyate sarvaṁ jagat sthāvara-jaṅgamam* ।
punar utpadyate yasmāt tad brahma liṅga-saṁjñākam ॥

— *Candrajñānāgama, Kriyāpāda*, 3.8

10. *līyate gamyate yatra yena caiva carācaram* ।
tadeva liṅgam ityukam liṅga-tattva-parāyaṇaiḥ ॥

—*Śivānubhava Sūtra*, 3.3

11. *līnam prapañcarūpaṁ hī sarvam etac carācaram* ।
sargādau gamyate yasmāt tasmāt liṅgam udīrītam ॥

— *Sūkṣmāgama, Kriyāpāda paṭala*, 6.6

12. *binduḥ śaktiḥ śivo nādaḥ śiva-śaktyātmakam jagat* ।

— *Candra-jñānāgama, Krīyāpāda, patala*, 3.13

13. *tasyaiva tejasā devī candrādi-graha-tārakāḥ* ।
prakāśante niyamitāḥ kāla-kṛptyā devāniśam ॥

— *Sūkṣmāgama, Kriyāpāda*, 6.9

14. *śruti-smrtyāgama-vihitatvena liṅga dhāranasya agnihotrādivat vaidikatvam siddham* ।

— *Śrīkarabhāṣya on BrS*, 1-1-1

15. *prāṇāpāna-samāghātāt kanda-madhyād yad utthitam* ।
prāṇa-liṅgaṁ tadākhyātam prāṇāpāna-nīrodhībhīḥ ।
prāṇo yatra layaṁ yāti tat prāṇaliṅgam uddiṣṭam ॥

— *SŚn*, 12.6 and 7

16. *bahu-janma-krtaih puṇyaih prakṣīṇe pāpa-pañjare* ।

śuddhāntaḥ-karaṇo dehī piṇḍa-śabdena gīyate ॥

— *Siddhānta Śikhāmaṇi*, V. 31

17. *aṁ iti brahma san-mātram gacchatiti gam-ucyate* ।
rūpyate'ṅgamiti prājnaiḥ aṅga-tattva, vicintakaih ॥

—*Śivānubhava Sūtra*, 4.4

18. *yathā ghṛte ghṛtam nyastaṁ, kṣīre ksīram jale jalam* ।
kevalatvam yathā prāptaṁ na kiñcridapi tad bhavet ॥

— Quoted from *EV*, p. 40

19. *atha vakṣyāmi girije śaiva-tattvāni vai śruṇu* ।
pañca-bhūtāni tanmātra-pañca karmendriyāṇī ca ॥
jñāna-karma-vībhāgena pañca-pañca vibhāgasaḥ ।
tvagādi-dhātavaḥ sapta pañca prāṇādi ॥
manaścāhaṅkṛtiḥ khyātir guṇā prakṛti-pūruṣāḥ
rago'vidyā kalā caiva nīyatiḥ kāla eva ca ।
māyā ca śuddha-vidyā ca maheśvara-sadāśivau ॥
śaktiśca śiva-tattvāni proktāni kramaśaḥ śrive ॥

— *Parameśvaragāma*, 2.17.29-33

20. *dīyate ca śiva-jñānam kṣīyate pāśa-bandhanam* ।
yasmād ataḥ samākhyātā dīkṣetīyaṁ vicakṣaṇaiḥ ॥

— *SŚn* (*Siddhānta Śikhāmaṇi*, 6-11)

21. *jñātvā devam mucyate sarva-pāśaiḥ-ityādiṣu-paraśiva-brahma jñānena-mala-trayātmaka-māyā-pāśa-duḥkha-nīvṛtti-pūrvaka-parama-puruṣārtha-paraśiva-tattva-prāpti-darśanāt* ।

— *ŚB*, II.5

22. *ataḥ mumukṣūṇām — bahu-janma tapaḥ-siddhāvyabhicāra bhaktireva sālokyādi-caturvidha-mukti-hetuḥ* ।

— *ŚB*, II.201

23. *bhāva-hīnas tathā yogī na śivaṁ draṣṭum īśvara* ।

— *ŚŚn*, 6-11

24. *nīḥspṛho'pi mahāyogī dharma mārgam ca na tyajet* ।

— *SŚn*, 16.9

25. *sivopāsaka-jīvan-muktānāṁ pracaṇḍātāpa-madhya-nīkṣipta-karpūra-dīpavad antaḥkaraṇa-sad-bhāve'pi sarva-śivātmaka jñāna-sadbhāvāt* ।

— *ŚB*, II.138

26. *sāṅkhyam yogaḥ pāñcarātraṁ vedāḥ pāśupatam tathā* ।
etāni mānabhūtāni nopahanyani yuktibhiḥ ॥
— *Siddhānta Śikhāmaṇi*, V.4

27. *liṅgācāraḥ sadācāraḥ śivācaras tathaiva ca* ।
bhṛtyācaro gaṇācāraḥ pañcācārāḥ pracoditāḥ ॥
— *Candra Jñānāgama, Kriyāpāda*, 9.4

28. *dharmārjitena dravyeṇa yat santarpaṇam anvaham* ।
guru-liṅga-jaṅgamānām sadācāraḥ sa vai smṛtaḥ ॥
— *op. cit.*, 9-6

29. *śiva-yogī śivaḥ sākṣād iti kaiṅkarya-bhakti taḥ* ।
pūjayed ādareṇaiva yathā liṅgam yathā gurum ॥
— *Siddhānta Śikhāmaṇi*, 9.9

7

Epilogue

THUS far we have considered how ancient *Śaiva* thinkers tried to comprehend the Reality (Śiva) and His relation with Man (*jīvātman*) and the world. Their speculations or thought-currents in these matters flowed through four channels:

1. Monism (*advaita*) : *KŚ* (Kāśmīr Śaivism)
2. Dualism-cum-monism (*dvaitādvaita*): Pāśupatism, Vīra-Śaivism
3. Pluralistic realism (*dvaita*) : Siddhānta Śaivism
4. Qualified monism (*viśiṣṭādvaita*): Śrīkaṇṭha's *Śivādvaita*

All these schools, however, belong to the 'Right-hand Path' (*dakṣiṇācāra*). There are other sects of Śaivism such as *Kāpālikas*, *Kālāmukhas*, Tāntric Śaivism and others. Due to their unacceptable practices, they are called 'Left-handed Path' (*vāmācara*). Some of them are briefly noted in the Appendix, as a detailed treatment will require a separate volume.

From the syncretic icons of Hari-Hara, Mārtaṇḍa-Bhairava, Ardha-nārīśvara found all over India, we may presume that such syncretic schools of Śaivism must have existed in olden times, but their treatises or literature is not easily available.

The Veda : the Āgama

Out of the above *dakṣiṇācāra* schools Pāśupatism (*pāś*) is based on the *Taittirīya Āraṇyaka* (17.1-5) and hence Vedic. The rest are based on *Āgamas* and are hence Āgamic.

Śaiva teachers claim equality of status between the *Veda* and *Āgamas*. They say that the *Āgama* contains the essence of the *Veda* (***vide supra***, p. 86). Śrīkaṇṭha's commentary on *Brahmasūtra* (*BrS*) and that of Śrīpati Paṇḍit (*Śrīkara Bhāṣya*) show that their respective sects. Śivādvaita and Vīra-Śaivism, though Āgamic, have Upaniṣadic support. Kauṇḍinya, the commentator of *Pāśupata Sūtra*, a work on Pāśupatism accepts that "Āgama is a *śāstra* that has come down from Maheśvara by *guru paraṁparā* (tradition of teachers).

āgamo nāma ā maheśvarād

guru-pāraṁparyāgatam śāstram

(*PāśSūtra* 5.8)

It is a pious belief to be respected.

Cosmopolitanism

Cosmopolitanism is a welcome feature of Āgamic Śaivism. It is a religion of the masses. In Pāśupatism *japa* of Vedic *mantras* automatically restricted its following to the classes who are eligible to study *Vedas*. But like Śrīkṛṣṇa's catholicity of outlook in *BG*, IX.32, the Āgamic Śaivism threw open the gates of *mokṣa* to women, śūdras and all low caste people. The *Śaiva Siddhāntin* saint Appār was a Veḷḷāḷ and saint Saṁbandhar was a brāhmaṇa. The high caste brāhmaṇa saint Sundraramūrti dined with non-brāhmaṇas and married a dancing girl (***supra***, pp. 64-69).

Influence of Brāhmaṇism

Some *Śaiva* sects show the influence of Brāhmaṇism,

probably due to local conditions. Thus *KŚ* claims superiority of Śaivism to *Veda*, and the *Trika* (*KŚ*) as being the best. But it laid down the condition that before being initiated to Śaivism all Vedic *saṁskāras* from Inception (*garbhādhāna*) to marriage must be performed (***vide supra***, p. 42).

It is interesting to find how a predominantly non-brāhmaṇa sect like Vīra-Śaivism assumes Brāhmaṇism *The Kāraṇāgama-Kriyāpāda, 3rd Paṭala* — a *Vīra-Śaiva Āgama* — requires a *Vīra-Śaiva* to perform *sandhyā*-prayer thrice a day. As in Brāhmaṇism, the *sandhyā* includes oblation of waters to the sun-god. *Japa* of the Śiva *Gāyatrī Mantra* and also performance of five sacrifices like daily *Pañca-mahā-yajñas* in Brāhmaṇism). Nandikeśvara, the author of the famous work "*Liṅga dhāraṇa-candrikā* claims that he was an exponent of a Vedic *Śakti Viśiṣṭādvaita* school."

The evolution of Vīra-Śaivism (***supra*** Ch. 6) explains this strong influence of Brāhmaṇism. *Vīra-Śaivas* up to the last generation, claimed that they were *Vīra-Śaiva Liṅgī Brāhmaṇas.*

The cosmopolitan Siddhānta Śaivism appears immune from such predominance of Brāmaṇism. Its *samayācāras* and *sanātanācāras* were both brāhmaṇas and non-brāhmaṇas and they inter-dined — a practice decribed by orthodox Brāhmaṇism.

Bhakti — the Path to Mokṣa

Śaiva sects differ from each other in the concept of *mokṣa* — especially the state of the individual soul in that state viz. complete merger with Śiva (as in *VŚ*) or retention of independent individuality. They, however, unanimously affirm *bhakti* (devotion to Śaiva) as **the** path to *mokṣa* and they prescribe it to their followers. Thus the entrant in Pāśupatism has to perform the *japa* of a *mantra* suitable to his stage, offer physical service to Śiva (and Śiva temple) and serve Śiva-Yogīs (***vide supra***, pp. 36-37). In Kāśmīr Śaivism, the elementary path, the *Āṇavopāya*, consists of *japa*, meditation. In a higher type of path to *mokṣa*, in *Śaktopāya*. *Mantra-japas* is emphasized (***vide supra***, pp. 51-52). The *Dāsa Mārga* and *Sakhā Mārga* in Siddhānta Śaivism correspond to the *dāsya* (service) and *sakhya* (intimacy, friendship) type of the ususal ninefold path of *bhakti* (***vide supra***, 78-79).

Śrīkaṇṭha is the first *Śaiva* teacher who proved that the theistic Śaivism of *Āgamas* has Upaniṣadic sanctions. He reconciled Vedic teaching with Āgamic theism — what may be called *Bhakti-karma-samuccaya* and exposition of *bhakti* as a path to *mokṣa* (***supra***, pp. 96-97).

In Vīra-Śaivism, the spiritual progress of an individual culminating in absorption in Śiva is neatly presented in *ṣaṭ-sthala*. The first *sthala* or stage of which is *Bhakta-sthala*. Śrīpati Paṇḍit prescribes listening to the glory of Śiva (*śravaṇa*) *japa* of Śiva's name, meditation and study of *Āgamas* in order to realize the blissful nature of Śiva.

It will thus be seen that despite some differences in details, all sects of Śaivism emphasize *bhakti*. The path to *mokṣa* is open to all.

This is why Śaivism has become the religion of the masses. The (Male) pastoral deities of western India such as Khaṇḍobā, Birobā, Nāikbā, etc. are forms of Śiva which masses worship and serve in their own way.

Yoga

Since Upaniṣadic times, practice of Yoga was in vogue in India. The technique in *sādhana pāda* in Patañjali's *Yoga Sūtra*, the eight steps (*aṅgas*) of the path of Yoga have been generally accepted by all whether it is Jainism, Buddhism or Brāhmaṇism, though Patañjali's philosophy is criticised by them. Yoga implies an attitude of detachment from worldly affairs (*saṁsāra*). It describes deep meditation for the realization of the *ātman*. Śiva is the supreme *yogī*. He is always absorbed in meditation and is detached even during his dance (***supra***, pp. 3-5). In Pāśupatism, the aspirant deliberately tries to emulate Śiva from smearing of ashes to the practice of *samādhi* in a lonely place or in a funeral ground. Kāśmīr Śaivism prescribed three paths (*upāyas*) to *mokṣa*, the higher types — the *Śākta* and *Śāṁbhava upāyas* — are practised at psychological level, the physical aspect of *Pātañjala Yoga* is ignored. The great *Siddhāntin*, *Śaiva* teacher Tirumūlar, in the third *Tantra* of *Tirumandiram*, describes Yoga. The terms are the same as those in Pātañjala Yoga but the fruit of mastering those *aṅgas* are totally different. For example, mastery over the first stage — *āsana* (posture) secures stay in Indra's capital (***vide supra***, p. 61). The special *Śaiva Yogas* viz. *khecarī*, *paryaṅka* and *candra* are different from *Pātañjala Yoga*.

After Tirumūlar, the *samayācāra* saints from Appār to Sundar Mūrti were ardent devotees. They did not encourage Yoga.

In the eleventh century AD the resurgence of *Viṣṇu-bhakti* movement (which boosted up *Śiva-bhakti* as well) and the political and social upheavals which followed, adversely affected the following of the Yoga path. It however, did survive as we find *Śiva-yogīs* even today.

Lastly, a modern reader will naturally ask: "Has Śaivism any relevance today?" The answer is "Yes. Positivly so."

The growing popularity of Yoga in advanced countries shows that people want some relief, mental peace from the tensions and imbalances created by the so-called advancement of science, technology and culture. Śaivism is a panacea to all these side-effects of modernism.

Śaivism boosts up the self-respect and self-confidence

of man. Asserts Śaivism:

> You are Śiva Himself. It is your privilege or birthright to be Śiva or Śiva-like again.

To a man worried with problems, this promise is an asset.

Śaivism further advises: "Though you are Śiva, your infinte powers are circumscribed due to your *mala* (dirt, i.e., *pāśa*). It can be washed off through ardent devotion to Śiva. Follow any path of *bhakti* (devotion) that you can afford. The merciful Śiva will favour you with divine Grace. Do your duty sincerely to the best of your ability and leave the rest with Lord Śiva."

This *Karma-bhakti-samuccaya* (synthesis of *niṣkāma karma* with ardent devotion) shall help you.

Yoga is possible for a selected few but *Karma-bhakti-samuccaya* is an easier way open to all to realize Śiva.

APPENDIX

Some Minor Sects of Śaivism

From literary, inscriptional, iconographic and other sources, we find that there were some other sects of Śaivism such as *Kāpālikas*, *Kālāmukhas*, *Hari-Hara*, *Ardha-nārīśvara* and *Nātha Panth*. Most of these were non-Vedic and were generally followed by people who were not eligible for Vedic studies. Unfortunately, with the exception of two or three sects not much information is available about their philosophy or — spiritual path. We shall briefly notice some of these sects.

Kāpālikas

The sect of Kāpālikas is also known as *kapālī, mahāvratin* and *soma-siddhāntins*. This sect appears to be an Āgamic branch of Pāśupatism. The followers of this sect carried *kapālas* or human skulls for begging alms. The sect came to be called Kāpālika due to this special characteristic of the followers. They were called *kāpālins* (bearers of a *kapāla*). Carrying a human skull was only a part of the *mahāvrata* which Śiva had to adopt in order to expiate for the sin of *brāhmaṇa-hatyā* viz. plucking off a head of god Brahmā. The observance of the *mahāvrata* considered of: (1) stay in a cremation ground or an isolated place, (2) smearing of the body with ashes from funeral pyres, (3) to carry *khaṭvānga* (skull-topped baton) and (4) use of human skull as a begging bowl.[1] The observers of this *mahāvrata* are *mahāvratins*.

The sect appears to be very old as the *Maitrī Upaniṣad* prohibits stay with them (*mantras* 7-8). The *Kūrma Purāṇa* (II.40.61-62) condemns it as being beyond the pale of the *Vedas* (*Veda bāhya*). Their caricatures in Sanskrit literature represents them to be hypocrites, and wicked. (For example, in Mahendra Varmā's *Matta-Vilāsa*, Bhavabhūti's *Mālatī-Mādhava*).

Originally they were devout followers of Śiva. As access to the *Vedas* was denied to them, they followed the path of *Āgamas*. Assuming the semblance of Śiva as a *mahāvratin* was a very difficult vow that they followed, despite the ridicule of the public at large. It is preposterous to believe that all these Āgamic followers of Śiva were condemnable simply because some of them might be following evil practices under the influence of Buddhists and *Tāntrikas*.

Kāpālika Philosophy

Few treatises on Kāpālika philosophy are available. Our information is based on unsympathetic sources who wanted to condemn the practices of a non-Vedic sect.

We can presume that like all other *Śaiva* sects, they believed in Śiva as the ultimate authority. Like all other schools of Indian philosophy (except the atheists) they regarded *mokṣa* (liberation from *saṁsāra*) as the ultimate goal (*puruṣārtha*) of human life. But their concept of *mokṣa* is **not** negative as *duḥkhānta* (end of miseries, a state wherein there is no misery). It is a bit strangely positive as implied in their epithet *soma-siddhāntin*. Out of this epithet, the term *soma* (– *sa* + *umā*) means 'Śiva in intimate-sexual-contact with Umā). And the 'greatest bliss' *mahāsukha* is the highest peak in sexual happiness. Those who believed in this *soma-siddhānta* were called *soma-siddhāntins*.

Rāmānuja in his *Śrī-bhāṣya* (a commentary on the *Brahma Sūtra*) informs us while commenting on *Patyurasāmañjasyāt* (*BrS*, 2.2.35) that Kāpālikas believe in God as the instrumental cause as against the Vedāntic view about Him as the material cause as well as the instrumental cause of the Universe. "They prescribe various rituals and ways of meditation and rules of conduct which were at variance with the Vedic ones. They prescribe various rituals and methods of meditation and rules of conduct repugnant to the Vedic ones." Applying six *mudrās* (marks) on the body and meditation on the *ātman* as abiding in *bhaga* is the way to *mokṣa*.[2] It may be noted that the term *bhaga* means *śūnya* in Buddhism and as such is not objectionable.

The Kāpālika teacher Bodholbaṇa Nityānanda (in *Śaṅkara Digvijaya*, Ch. 3) explains:

> Our way of life confers happiness to all as it is without formal rituals. For ritualistic actions do not lead to *mokṣa*. We adore only Bhairava (i.e., Śiva), the creator, sustainer and destroyer of all. All deities obey Him.

This in a nutshell is the Kāpālika philosophy.

B. Bhattacharya in *Esoteric Buddhism* tells us that the sect came under the influence of Buddhism. Later it was dominated by Śāktism and adopted five *makāras* in the literal sense of the terms. They revelled in *makāras* like *madya* (wine), *māṁsa* (meat), *maithuna* (sexual intercourse) as a pathway to *mokṣa*. Naturally it became unpopular despite their bluff of possessing miraculous powers.

Kālāmukha Sect

Kālāmukha was a branch (with some changes) of the ancient Pāśupata sect. They were so-called as they used a black line(s) on the forehead (T.A. Gopinathrao). The sect spread over the major part of Karnataka and some part of Andhra. It had two branches: (i) *Śakti Pariṣad* and (ii) *Siṁha Pariṣad*. *Śakti Pariṣad* dominated in Dharwar and Shimoga districts. Inscriptions from Bījāpur (AD 1074-75). Muttagi (AD 1147, 1158) indicate that Kāśmīr brāhmaṇas were the exponents or preachers of this sect. They were experts in *Lakulāgam* (Pāśupatism) but they also taught *Vedas*, *Śāstras*, *Purāṇas* in the *maṭhs* (monasteries) attached to their *Śiva-liṅga* temples. They emphasized Yoga. The Kings of Karnataka and Andhra supported their temple-institutions generously as can be seen from Kannaḍa inscriptions from the eleventh, twelfth and the early half of the thirteenth centuries AD.

Modern scholars believe it to be an earlier form of Vīra-Śaivism on the following grounds:

1. All important temples and *maṭhs* and sacred places of Kālāmukhas are slowly and imperceptibly absorbed into Vīra-Śaivism. (S.C. Nandimath —*Handbook— Vīra-Śaivism*, p. 9).

2. Mysore Gazetteer (II. Part 11, 885) states: "The Śaivite revival under Bāsava and the early *Vīra-Śaivas* seem to have followed as the natural result of the work of these *Śaiva*

teachers of the Pāśupata (*sic* for Kālāmukha school of Belagami — Belagave).

3. The term *jaṅgama* — now used for the priest-class among *Vīra-Śaivas* was applied to Kālāmukha teachers. For example, Gadag inscription of AD 1192, Kālāmukha teacher Candrabhūṣana Paṇḍit is called '*Jaṅgama-liṅga* of Lord Trikūṭeśvara'. Sarveśvaradeva, Kālāmukha head of Jagdīśvara temple Munavalli, is called *Jaṅgama Liṅgāvatāra* in the inscription of AD 1252.

Very little is recorded about their philosophy. Kaunteya Muni, a Kālāmukha teacher of Hombal is credited with the view: "Śiva-Brahman, though formless can by its will-power create, sustain and destroy the world."

A view endorsed by Revaṇārya and other teachers of Vīra-Śaivism.

These Pāśupata (Kālāmukha) brāhmaṇas seem to have contributed their mite in the formation of Vīra-Śaivism.

SOME SYNCRETIC ICONS

Hari-Hara

Since Purāṇic times attempts have been made to combine (or reduce the rivalry between) followers of the powerful sects of Śaivism and Vaiṣṇavism. Thus we find the *Kūrma Purāṇa* declaring the identity of Śiva and Viṣṇu. States the *Kūrma Purāṇa* (I.15.89-91):

> He who is Viṣṇu is Rudra himself. And he who is Rudra is Janārdana.[3]

The *Nārada*, a *Vaiṣṇava Purāṇa* tells : (83.23) "Originally there was god Kṛṣṇa who divided himself into two, the right part was Viṣṇu and the left Mahādeva". The *Matsya Purāṇa* (259.22.27) gives instruction for the preparation of a Hari-Hara icon of which the right part is *Śaiva* while the left half is *Vaiṣṇava*. Thus half part of the head has matted hair with the crescent moon while the left half of the head has a bejewelled crown. That way the whole body showed both *Śaiva* and *Vaiṣṇava* characteristics. Curiously enough, it was the Turkish, i.e., Kuṣāṇa King Huviṣka (AD 106-138) who attempted a compromise between the two sects by using such complex figure on his coins. If this icon represents a sect, the sect must be presumed to have existed at those places or states where they are found. We find such icons at Visnagar (Gujarat), Sopara (Thane district, Maharashtra), Tirupati (in Andhra Pradesh) was a Śiva-icon Vaiṣṇavised at the time of

Rāmānuja. Old Aḷwār saints like Payalvar, Paugai regard Tirupati as both Śiva and Viṣṇu.[4] The icon of Viṭṭhala at Paṇḍharpur (Maharashtra) is also believed to combine both Śiva and Viṣṇu. As it can be seen from legend this Hari-Hara cult most probably began from the *Mahābhārata* period.

Mārtaṇḍa-Bhairava

The *Skanda-Purāṇa, Khaṇḍa* VII contains a list of Śiva-Āditya Liṅgas. I think a featureless *liṅga* is not an icon or idol. Those being nor icons are not called Mārtaṇḍa-Bhairava (the Sun-Śiva complex). We find such icons in east India (Bengal, Orissa). The *Liṅga-Purāṇa Uttarārdha* in 16.27-39 states that paying obeisance to Śiva is the same as done unto the Sun-god.[5] Not much is known about this sect.

Nātha-Pantha[6]

This important cult has been carefully studied by Eastern and Western scholars like Rāhul Sānkrityāyan, Hazārī Prasād Dvivedī, G.W. Briggs and others. This *Pantha* seems to be influenced by Buddhist *Sahajayāna* and *Vajrayāna* cults, 'Left-hand' *Śaiva* cults like Kāpālika, Kaul and also by *Śaiva Āgamas*. It is noted for its Yogic culture. Assimilation of Buddhist concept of *śūnya*, *sahaja* and *Śiva-Śakti* concept of Āgamic Śaivism seems to have been fused together in this cult. The *guru-paraṁparā* of this sect includes the names of Tibetan (Buddhist *siddhas*). This fusion seems to have taken place during AD 800-1100. It is after AD 1100 that an independent *Nātha Pantha* became established and is respected all over India as a *Śaiva* sect. Its followers too assumed some externalities of Śiva like smearing with ashes, using *ḍamaru* (hand-drum) etc. Some *Santa-paraṁparās* (traditions of saints) in Mediaeval India have been developed out of this sect). It is a living sect with affluent centres in various parts of the country.

Notes

1. *śīraḥ kapālī dhvajavān bhikṣāsī karma vedayan* ।
   brahma-hā dvādaśāhdāni mitabhuk śuddhīmāpnuyāt ॥
   — *Yājñavalkya Smṛti*, 3.2.42

   This is echoed in *Kūrma Purāṇa*, II.30.12-16
2. *Śrībhāṣya* on *BrS*, 2.2.35 (Karamarkar's translation pp. 690-91.
3. *yo viṣṇuḥ sa svayaṁ rudro*

yo rudraḥ sa janārdanaḥ ।

— *Kūrma Purāṇa,* I.15.89-91

4. C.V. Narayana Aiyar, *The Early History of Śaivism in South India*, Madras University, Madras, 1936, pp. 240-42.
5. *namaḥ śivaya devāya . . . tubhyaṁ brahmane sūrya — mūrtaye* ।

— *Liṅga Purāṇa*, II.16.27-60

6. Based on *Tattvajñāna Mahākośa*, Pune, 1974 and G.V. Tagare, "Jñāneśvara and Vajrayāna sect", in *Navabharat* (Monthly) Pune, August 1956.

Glossary

Ābhāsavāda (in *KŚ*) : Absolute self-dependence of Śiva: *Śiva's svātantrya.*

Ābhoga (in *KŚ*) : Spiritual delight. Also called *camatkāra.*

A-cit : Non-intelligent, non-spirit.

Acintyatva : Incomprehensibility.

Adhiṣṭhāna : Substratum, base.

Adhiṣṭhātṛ : The presiding principle.

Adho-māyā (in *SŚ*) : *Aśuddha-māyā.*

Adhyāsa : False superimposition.

Adhvā : Pathway, course. *Śuddha adhvā* — The intrinsic course super-mundane manifestation; *aśuddha adhvā* — The course of mundane manifestation.

Advaita : Monism.

Āgama : Scriptural Text — Śiva, the author.

Agnihotra : Maintenace of sacred fire.

Ahaṅkāra or *ahantā* : 'I'-ness; I-consciousness; Ego.

Ajñāna : The primal limitation (*mala* or *pāśa*), inherent in man.

Ānanda : Supreme Bliss.

Ānanda upāya : The same as *anupāya.*

Ananta (in *SŚ*): The representative agent of cosmic functions: A mature soul free from practically all bonds.

Āṇava mala : Primal limiting condition which reduces the Śiva-like powers of *jīvātman*.

Āṇava upāya : The yoga whereby the individual utilizes his senses *prāṇa* and *manas* for self-realization. Also called *bhedopāya, kriyā yoga* or *kriyopāya*.

Aṅga (in *VŚ*) : An individual (soul) trying for union with Śiva.

Aṇu (in *KŚ*) : One that breathes; the limited experient.

Anugraha : Grace; A function of Śiva; Śiva's grace essential for *mokṣa*.

Anupāya (in *KŚ*) : Spontaneous manifestation of Śiva without any special effort.

Anusandhāna : Repeated intensive awareness of essential Reality (i) A synthetic unity of apperception (ii) spiritual experiences, (iii) Concentration on natural *so'ham* sound.

Apāna : Inhalation.

Araṇi : The piece of wood for kindling fire by attrition.

Asat : Non-being.

Aśuddha vidyā : Empirical knowledge (limited to a few particulars).

Āvaraṇa : Veil; covering. But in *VŚ*, protecti ve armour (*rakṣā kavaca*). These are eight in number viz. *suru, liṅga, aṅgama, pādodaka, bhasma, rudrākṣa* and *mantra*.

Avidyā : Non-knowledge; ignorance.

Avikalpa (*nirvikalpa*) : Direct *jñāna* — Direct realization of Reality, unparticularised awareness.

Avyabhicāritva : Non-presence of the one without the other.

Bandha : Bondage, *pāśa*, limited knowledge.

Bhairava : *Para Bhairava* : Śiva; *Apara Bhairava* : Siddha.

Bhairavī mudrā : A special *mudrā* with attention inward and gaze outward.

Bhakti : Devotion : *Parā bhakti* : A higher type of devotion.

Bhāvanā : Creative contemplation (in *śākta upāya*).

Bhoga : Experience; *Bhoktā*: Experient.

Bhūta : Gross physical element.

Bhuvana : Planes or place of existence there are 108 *bhāvanās* in Śaivism.

Bindu : A metaphysical point, (a compact mass of Śakti ready to create).

Brahma-randhra : The *sahasrāra carka* : An aperture in the crown of the head.

Caitanya : The foundational consciousness endowed with the *jñāna* and *kriyā*.

Cakra : (i) Collection of Śaktis; (ii) Yogic plexus such as *mūlādhāra, anāhata*.

Camatkāra (in *KŚ*) : Bliss of pure I-consciousness.

Cit : Foundational consciousness; Intelligent.

Citi (in *KŚ*) : Absolute's consciousness-power (for world process).

Citta : The mind (of an empirical individual).

Darśana : A school of philosophy; Insight.

Dehātmaikya-bhāva : Notion of the identity of the body and soul.

Dhāraṇā : Concentration (on something); Meditation.

Dharma : (i) an Attribute; (ii) Disposition of intellect to good; (iii) Good predicative element.

Dhvani : A subtle sound; *Anāhata nāda*.

Dhyāna yoga : Yoga of meditation; (in *KŚ*) The highest *dhāraṇā* in *āṇava upāya*.

Dīkṣā : Initiation; The ceremony is a gift of and entrance into a spiritual path. The procedure of a *dīkṣā* varies with different sects.

Divya mudrā : *Khecarī mudrā*.

Dṛk-kriyā-śakti : The power of knowledge and action (inherent unto *jīvātman*).

Dvaita : Pluralistic Realism; Dualism.

Dvaitādvaita : Dualism-cum-monism.

Gaṇatattva (in *SŚ*) : The principle of material constituent.

Ghorā śaktis : The Śakti-deities that drag the Jīva to *saṁsāra*.

Gocarī : '*Go*' means 'a sense-organ'. They are related to *antaḥkaraṇa;* (in *KŚ*) A sub-species of Vāmeśvarī.

Haṁsa : The *jīva*; The soul.

Haṁsa-japa: The consciousness of *nāda-kalā*; The *ajapā japa*.

Icchā : Will, will-power to do anything; *Icchā-Śakti* (in *KŚ*): The innate power of *parama* Śiva, the onward state of Śiva wherein *jñāna* and *kriyā* are unified; the predominant aspect of Sadāśiva. The sovereign free-will is Śiva's *svātantrya*.

Idantā : 'This-ness'; objective consciousness.

Īśvarādvaya-vāda : The doctrine of non-difference between man and soul.

Īśvara-tattva: The fourth *tattva* from Śiva, *jñāna* is predominant (in *aham-idam* relation) (also in *KŚ*).

Jagadānanda : The bliss of the Divine (in *KŚ*); cf. Śivānanda (in *VŚ*).

Jagat : The world.

Jāgrat (*avasthā*): The waking condition (*jñāna*); Objective knowledge in waking condition.

Jīva : The individual soul: classified according to *malas*, associated: *vijñānākala* (with *āṇavamala*) *pralayākala* (with *āṇava* and *kārma malas*) *sakala* (with *āṇava*, *kārma, māyīya malas*).

Jīvan-mukta : The liberated individual soul while alive

Jīvan mukti : The experience of the above state.

Jñāna : Spiritual knowledge; (in *KŚ*) limited knowledge, a source of bond.

Jñāna yoga : *Śākta upāya.*

Kalā : (i) Part, particle; (ii) A *kañcuka* limiting *jīva*'s activity.

Kalā-cakra : *Mātṛcakra*. The group of letters from *a* to *kṣa.*

Kāla tattva : Time, past, present and future.

Kañcuka : Coverings of *māyā* converting Śiva into *jīva*. They are (1) *kalā* (2) [*aśuddha*] *vidyā* (3) *rāga*, (4) *niyati*, (5) *kāla*.

Karaṇa : The means of *jñāna* and *kriyā*. Thus *antaḥkaraṇa* is 'internal organ'; psychic apparatus. *Bahiṣkaraṇa* — External organ.

Khecarī (in *SŚ*) : The special yoga propounded by Tirumular in *Tirumandiram.*

Khecarī mudrā or *Śivāvasthā* (in *KŚ*) : Śiva-like bliss.

Khyāti : Knowledge.

Kleśa : Hindrance; Impurity (*SŚ*) *kṣetrajña*; The individual soul; The empirical subject.

Kriyā (in *KŚ*) : Power to create everything out of oneself, also called *śuddha vidyā.*

Kṛtya : (1) Action; (2) Function — the five functions of Śiva are: viz. *sṛṣti* (manifestation, creation), *sthiti* (maintenance of the manifested), *saṁhāra* (withdrawal of the manifestation), *vilaya* or *pidhāna* (veiling of self), *anugraha* (grace).

Kumbhaka : Retention of breath in *prāṇāyāma* (breath-control).

Kuṇḍalinī : The spiritual *śakti* lying in three and half folds in the *mūlādhāra cakra*.

Laya : Dissolution, complete concentration.

Liṅga : (i) Representation of Śiva; (ii) The *Brahman* (iii) varities of *liṅgas*: (a) *mukha-liṅga* (with face of Śiva on the *liṅga,* (b) *vigraha liṅga* (with full form of Śiva on the *liṅga*, (c) *sthāṇu* (faceless *liṅgas*).

Madhya : *Suṣumnā*, central *prāṇa nāḍī*.

Madhyamā : **See** *parā vāk*.

Mahāmāyā/Māyā: Deluding power: It is *śuddha* or *mahāmāyā* having contact with Śiva. In *SŚ māyā* is the independent creator of the world : *Mahāmāyā* or (*aparā*) is below *śuddha vidyā*. *Māyā* is the material substratum of the cosmos.

Mantra : Sacred formula for chanting.

Mantreśvara : The individual who realize Śiva, Śiva assigns some duties to them.

Mārga (in *SŚ*) : Pathway to *mokṣa*. They are four:

(1) *Dāsa-marga :* service unto Śiva and *Śivabhaktas*.

(2) *Sat-putra mārga* : Service to Śiva as father.

(3) *Sakhā-mārga* : Service as a friend of *sakhya bhakti*.

(4) *San-mārga* : The path of knowledge.

Mātṛkā : The letters of alphabet and word power (of these deities).

Māyīya mala : A bond created by *māyā*.

Moha : Delusion.

Mudrā : Yogic control of certain organs or postures of hands, etc.

Mukti or *Mokṣa* : Liberation from *saṁsara*.

Nāda : (i) Metaphysics: The first movement of Śiva-Śakti to manifestation; (ii) In yoga: *anāhata* sound experienced in meditation.

Nāḍī : Nostril throughwhich the breath flows : Sūrya or Iḍā (right nostril), Soma or Piṅgalā (left nostril).

Nididhyāsana: Continuous contemplation: intuitive realization.

Nīmeṣa : Lit. closing of eyelids; (in *KŚ*) Dissolution of the object into the subject (the inner activity of *spanda*).

Nīmīlana samādhī (in *KŚ*) : Absorption of the individual consciousness into universal consciousness.

Nimitta-kāraṇa : Efficient cause.

Nirākāra : Formless; (in *SŚ*) Possession of all forms.

Nirvikalpa : Devoid of all ideation.

Niṣkala :Formless, pure.

Niyati : The principle of determination of *karmas*.

Pañca-kṛtya : ***See under*** *kṛtya*.

Pañcākṣara (in *VŚ*) : The *mantra* — *śivāya namaḥ*.

Pañca-śakti : The five fundamental *śaktis* of Śiva viz. *cit*, *ānanda, icchā, jñāna* and *kriyā*.

Parāmarśa : Mental grasping; contemplation; Remembrance.

Parāpara (in *KŚ*) : The intermediate stage both identical and different.

Parā vāk : The first stage of speech at the *mūlādhāra cakra*: *Paśyanti* is a more manifest stage (place heart region), *madhyamā* is inarticulate speech (at the throat region), *vaikharī*: articulate, gross, physical words.

Pāśa : Bondage : they are the *āṇava, kārma* and *mayīya*.

Paśu : The empirical individual bound by *avidyā*.

Pati : Lord Śiva, the liberated soul.

Piṇḍa (in *VŚ*) : An individual in the last (pre-*mokṣa*) birth.

Prakāśa Lit : Light; Śiva's omniscience.

Pralayākala : ***See under*** *jīva*.

Pramā : Exact knowledge.

Pramāṇa : Means of knowledge.

Pramātṛ : Knower.

Prameya : Knowable, object of knowledge.

Pratybhijña : Recognition.

Puruṣa ajñāna : Innate ignorance of *puruṣa* about real self.

Pūryaṣṭaka : *Liṅga-śarīra* (subtle body) of eight constituents viz. five *tanmātras, buddhi, ahaṁkāra* and *manas* (mind).

Rāga : A *kañcuka* of *māyā* creating desire, passion.

Rajas : A constituent or quality of *pakṛti*, shows activity.

Śabda : Sound; Word.

Śabda Brahma : The *Veda*s, the ultimate reality wherein thought and word are identical.

Ṣaḍadhvā (in *KŚ*) : Six forms of manifestation : *mantra, varṇa* and *pada* on the subjective side and *kalā, tattva* and *bhuvana*s on the objective side.

Sadāśiva or *Sādākhya* : The third devolutionary *tattvas* from Śiva (on the evolution of the world); (in *VŚ*) One of the five Śiva *tattvas*, evolved from *bindu*.

Sahaja vidyā : Knowledge of the innate essential nature; Sometimes *unmanī avasthā*.

Śākta upāya or *Śāṁbhava upāya* : **See under** *Upāya*.

Śakti : Divine will power (to create, sustain and annihilate the world; (ii) The *spanda*, creative pulsation of Śiva.

Śakti-pāta : Descent of *Śakti*; Divine grace (for self-realization).

Sāmarasya (in *KŚ*) : Union of Śiva and Śakti identical stage with disappearance of differences.

Samāveśa : Being possessed by the Divine; Absorption of one's consciousness in the Divine.

Saṁsāra : Transmigratory existence; the world process.

Saṁvit : Consciousness; supreme consciousness with complete fusion of *prakāśa* and *vimarśa; jñāna śakti*.

Ṣaṭ-sthala (in *VŚ*) : Stages of spiritual development viz. (1) *Bhakta*, (2) *Maheśvara*, (3) *Prasādi*, (4) *Prāṇa-liṅga*, (5) *Śaraṇa*, (6) *Aikya sthala*.

Ṣaṭsthala : Also *Sthala*. Spiritual position of a *jīva*.

Spanda : Creative pulsation of Śiva.

Sthūla śarīra : Gross physical body.

Śuddha adhvā : The course of world manifestation from Śiva to *śuddha vidyā*, the fifth *tattva* wherein consciousness of both 'I' and 'The world' is equally prominent.

Sūkṣma śarīra : **See** *Pūryaṣṭaka;* subtle body.

Śūnya (Buddhism) : An indefinable state of Reality (ii) (Śaiva) A state wherein no object is experienced.

Svātantrya : Absolute freedom of will, the *vimarśa śakti.*

Tamas (Lit.) : Darkness; a constituent of *prakṛti*, principle of delusion.

Tan-mātra : 'That only', subtle element (of gross *pṛthivī*, etc. or of sense-perception such as *śabda, sparśa*).

Tantra : A system of philosophy.

Tattva : 'Thatness', principle, a category (e.g., in *Sāṅkhya* evolution of the universe).

Tirodhāna : Śiva's power to conceal.

Trika : System of philosophy of Triad such as *nara, śakti, śiva, pati, paśu pāśa* — Kāśmīr Śaivism.

Tūrya : The fourth state of consciousness beyond those of waking, dream, sleep. It strings these states together.

Tūryātīta : State beyond the above state of pure blissfulness.

Uccāra (in *KŚ*) : A technique of concentration on prāṇa.

Udāna : Upward moving vital *vāyu*; (ii) The *śakti* moving upward in *suṣumnā* after awakening.

Udyama (in *KŚ*) : The sudden spontaneous emergence of supreme I-consciousness.

Unmeṣa (in *KŚ*) : The emergence of divine I-consciousness; The start of the world-process.

Upādāna kāraṇa : The material cause.

Upāya (in *KŚ*) : Pathway to liberation. They are (i) *anupāya*, (ii) *saṁbhava*, (iii) *śākta*, (iv) *āṇava*.

Vāha : Flow of breath: The channel of *prāṇa* flowing through nostrils.

Vaikharī : Overt articulate speech; ***See Parā vāk***.

Varṇa : A letter of alphabet; *anāhata* (unstruck) *nāda* (sound).

Vāsanā : Residual trace of action and impressions in mind.

Vidyā : (i) *Śuddha vidyā tattva*; (ii) Limited knowledge a *kañcuka* of *māyā*.

Vikalpa : Option; Difference of perception; thought-construct.

Vijñānākala : Individual soul free from *kārma* and *māyīya mala*.

Vimarśa : Self-consciousness of *parama* Śiva fall of *jñāna* and *kriyā* for world process.

Vyāpti : Universal relation; concommitance.

Yoga : Joining or communion with God; *Samādhi* — there is no mental fluctuation in this state.

Yoni : Source, womb; (in *KŚ*), Nine classes of consonants.

Bibliography

Abhinava Gupta : *Tantra-sāra*, Kashmir Sanskrit Series (*KSS*), Śrīnagar, 1918.

———, *Tantrāloka* (with Jayaratha's Com. (= commentary): *KSS*.

———, *Paramārtha-sāra* (Com. by Yogarāja) : *KSS* 7, 1916.

Ādyanātha : *Anuttara-pañcāsīkā* : *KSS* 14, 1918.

Āgama-Ardha-māgadhī : Agamodaya Samiti, Bombay.

Āgama-Pāli-Bauddha : Nalanda edition, ed. by Jagadish Kaśyapa.

Aiyer C.V. Narayan : *Origin and Early History of Śaivism in South India*, University of Madras, 1936.

Awaliker Pandit (ed.) : *Viveka Cintāmaṇi* (Marathi), Dharwar, 1963.

Bhagavatī Sūtra (Ardha Māgadhī-Jain canon) : tr. by Pt. Bechardas, Gujarat Vidyapeeth, Ahmedabad.

Bhandarkar, R.G. : *Vaiṣṇavism and Śaivism* (A Symposium) Bhandarkar O.R. Institute, Pune, 1976.

Bharatiya Vidya Bhavan : *Vedic Age* (*History and Culture of Indian People*), Bombay, 1965.

Bhāsarvajña : *Ratna Ṭīkā* (on *Gaṇa Kārikā*), C.D. Dalal, 1920.

Bhojadeva : *Tattva-prakāśa* (with com. *Tattvadīpikā*), ed. by T. Ganapatiśāstrī, Trivandrum, 1920.

Chakrobarti, Haripad : *Pāśupata Sūtram* (Eng. Translation), Academic Publishers, Calcutta, 1970.

Chatterji J.C. : *Kashmir Shaivism*: Kashmir Granth Mala, Śrīnagar, 1914.

Coomaraswami A. : *Dance of Śiva*, Asia, Bombay, 1948.

Dandge G.B. : *Rudra, Yajña and Śiva Liṅga* (Marathi), Maharashtra Granth Bhandar, Kolhapur.

Dasgupta S.N. : *History of Indian Philosophy,* Vol. V, Motilal Banarsidass, Delhi, 1975.

Gajendragadkar K.V. : *Neo-Upaniṣadic Philosophy*, Bharatiya Vidya Bhavan, Bombay, 1959.

Hāla (Sātavāhana) : *Gāthā Saptaśatī* (Marathi), tr. by S.A. Joglekar, Pune.

Haradatta : *Gaṇa Kārikā*, C.D. Dalal, 1920.

Haribhadra : *Ṣaḍ-darśana-saṅgraha*, Bhāratī Jñānapīṭha, 1970.

Hastings : *Encyclopaedia of Religion and Ethics.*

Jash, Prabanananda: *History of Shaivism*, Roy and Choudhuri, Calcutta, 1974.

Kāravāṇa Māhātmya (Purāṇic) : ed. by C.D. Dalal, 1920.

Kṣemarāja : *Parā-praveśikā*, KSS, 1918.

———, *Pratyabhijña-hṛdaya*, ed. by Jayadev Singh, Motilal Banarsidass, Delhi, 1980.

Lakulīśa : *Pāśupata sūtra*, (with Kauṇḍinya's Com.) ed. by Ananta Kṛṣṇa Śāstrī, Trivandrum, 1940.

Lorensen David N.: *The Kāpālikas and Kālāmukhas*, Thomson Press, New Delhi, 1972.

Madhva : Com. on *Brahmasūtra* (with com. *Tattva Prakāśikā*), Marathi Translation, Rangacharya Raddi, Pune, 1949.

Maheśvarānanda : *Mahārtha-Mañjarī*, Yoga Tantra Granthmālā, Vārāṇasī, 1972.

Malldevaru H.P. : *Essentials of Vīraśaivism*, Bharatiya Vidya Bhavan, Bombay, 1973.

Marshall, Sir John : *Mohenjo Daro and the Indian Civilization*, 3 vols., London, 1931.

Nandikeśvara : *Liṅga-dhāraṇa-candrikā*, ed. by M.R. Sakhare, Belgaum, 1938.

Nandimath S.C. : *A Handbook of Vīraśaivism*, Dharwar, 1942.

Pande K.C.: *Abhinavagupta: An Historical and Philosophical Study*, Chowkhamba Sanskrit Series, Benaras, 1935.

———, *Bhāskarī*, Vol. I, III, Lucknow University.

Pandit B.N. : *Aspects of Kashmir Śaivism*, Utpala Pub., Śrīnagar, 1977.

Patañjali : *Vyākaraṇa-mahā-bhāṣya*, ed. by Keilhorn.

Purāṇas : Guru Mandal edition, Calcutta.

Pusalkar A.D. : *Studies in Epics and Puranas of India*, Bharatiya Vidya Bhavan, Bombay, 1963.

Radhakrishnan S. (ed.) : *History of Philosophy — Eastern and Western*, Vol. I, George Allan & Unwin, London, 1967.

Ramakrishna Mission : *Cultural Heritage of India*, Vol. IV, Calcutta, 1956.

Rāmānuja : *Śrī-bhāṣya* (on *Brahma sūtra*), tr. by R.D. Karamarkar, Pune University, Pune.

Rao T. Gopinath : *Essentials of Hindu Iconography*, Motilal Banarsidass, Delhi.

Renou L. : *L'inde Classique*, (French).

Sachau S.C. : *Alberuni's India*, London, 1910.

Sakhare M.R. : *History and Philosophy of Lingayat Religion*, Belgaum, 1942.

Śaṅkara : *Śārīraka Bhāṣya* (on *Brahma Sūtra*), Nirnaya Sagara, Bombay, 1904.

Śivayogi Śivācārya : *Siddhānta Śikhāmaṇi*, Vīraśaiva Sāhitya Saṁśodhana Maṇḍal, Śolāpur, 1990.

Smṛtis : Guru Mandal edition, Calcutta.

Srīkaṇṭha : *Brahma-mīmāṁsā-bhāṣya* : ed. by Halasyanāth Śastrī, Kumbhakoṇam, vol. I 1908, vol. II 1918.

Śrinivasachari P.N. : *Philosophy of Bhedābheda*, Madras, 1950.

Śrīpati Paṇḍit : *Śrīkara Bhāṣya* (on *Brahmasūtra*) ed. by C. Hayavadanrao, Bangalore, 1937.

Somānanda : *Śiva-dṛṣṭi*, *KSS* 54, 1934.

Sūryanārāyaṇa Śāstrī : *Śivādvaita of Śrīkaṇṭha*, Madras University, 1930 and 1972.

Tagare G.V. : *Śaivadarśana* (Marathi) Continental, Pune, 1987.

Upaniṣat-Saṅgraha : ed. by J.L. Shastri, Motilal Banarsidass, Delhi, 1970.

Utpala-deva : *Iśvara-pratyabhijñā* (Com. by Abhinava-gupta) vol. I, KSS 22, 1918; vol. II, KSS 33, 1921.

Vasugupta : *Śivasūtra* ed. and tr. (Marathi) by G.V. Tagare, Impressions, Belgaum, 1996.

———, *Spanda Kārikā*, ed. and tr. (Marathi) by G.V. Tagare, Satara, 1984.

Vedas : Svādhyāya Maṇḍala, Aundh.

Vyāsa : *Kūrmapurāṇa*, A.S. Gupta, Kashiraj Trust, Vārāṇasī, 1972.

———, *Bhagavad Gītā* (with 18 commentaries), Gujarati Printing Press, Bombay.

———, *Brahmāṇḍa Purāṇa*, tr. (Eng.) by G.V. Tagare, Motilal Banarsidass, Delhi.

———, *Mahābhārata*, Gita Press, Gorakhpur.

———, *Mahā-Śiva-Purāṇa*, Pandit Pustakalaya, Vārāṇasī, Saṁvat 2020.

Index

Index